PERSONALISATION

Peter Beresford,
with responses from Sarah Carr, Jim Main, Alan Roulstone,
Pat Stack, Helga Pile, Roddy Slorach and Colin Slasberg

SERIES EDITORS:
Iain Ferguson and Michael Lavalette

This print edition first published in Great Britain in 2014 by

Policy Press
University of Bristol
6th Floor
Howard House
Queen's Avenue
Bristol BS8 1SD
UK
t: +44 (0)117 331 5020
f: +44 (0)117 331 5367
pp-info@bristol.ac.uk
www.policypress.co.uk

North American office:
Policy Press
c/o The University of Chicago Press
1427 East 60th Street
Chicago, IL 60637, USA
t: +1 773 702 7700
f: +1 773-702-9756
e:sales@press.uchicago.edu
www.press.uchicago.edu

ISBN 978 1 44731 614 5 paperback

British Library Cataloguing in Publication Data
A catalogue record for this book is available from the British Library.

Library of Congress Cataloging-in-Publication Data
A catalog record for this book has been requested.

Cover design Policy Press
Printed in Great Britain by www.4edge.co.uk

OTHER TITLES AVAILABLE IN THIS SERIES

POVERTY AND INEQUALITY by Chris Jones and Tony Novak

ADULT SOCIAL CARE by Iain Ferguson and Michael Lavalette

MENTAL HEALTH by Jeremy Weinstein

ETHICS by Sarah Banks

CHILDREN AND FAMILIES by Paul Michael Garrett

For more information about this series visit: www.policypress.co.uk/crdsw.asp

Policy Press also publishes the journal *Critical and Radical Social Work*; for more information visit: http://www.policypress.co.uk/journals_crsw.asp

Contents

Notes on contributors

Lead author

Peter Beresford is Professor of Social Policy and the Director of the Centre for Citizen Participation at Brunel University. He is also the chair of Shaping Our Lives, the national disabled people's and service users' organisation and network. He is a regular contributor to the *Guardian* and *Community Care*.

Respondents

Following a successful career with the Social Care Institute for Excellence (SCIE), **Sarah Carr** founded an independent mental health and social care knowledge consultancy. She is an Honorary Senior Lecturer at Institute for Applied Social Studies at the University of Birmingham, a Visiting Fellow of the Centre for Government and Charity Management at London South Bank University and a Fellow of the Royal Society of Arts. Sarah is also a trustee of the National Survivor and User Network (NSUN) and a member of the editorial board of the journal *Disability and Society*. (See more at: www.thementalelf.net/author/sarah-carr/#sthash.sddMw652.dpuf)

Jim Main is a practitioner and trade union activist in Scotland.

Alan Roulstone is Professor of Disability Studies at Leeds University. His recent books include (with S. Prideaux) (2012) *Understanding disability policy*, Bristol:, Policy Press, and (with H. Bish-Mason) (eds) (2012) *Disability hate crime and violence*, Oxford: Routledge.

Pat Stack works for Disability in Camden (DIUSC) and chairs the London Self-Directed Support Forum. He writes here in a personal capacity.

—

Helga Pile is the trade union UNISON's national officer for social care.

Roddy Slorach is a researcher and service user activist in London

Colin Slasberg qualified as a social worker in the 1970s. His 40-year career has spanned practice in adult and children's services, management of practice, operational management, strategic planning and independent consultancy. He led a successful five-year project as an assistant director in a unitary council to develop an outcome- based approach to practice and commissioning as a way to personalise social care. He has had a number of papers published – both singly and with others – including on: implementation of outcome-based working; how the current personal budget strategy is failing; and creating a fit-for-purpose approach to eligibility.

Series editors

Iain Ferguson is Professor of Social Work and Social Policy at the University of the West of Scotland and a member of the Steering Committee of the Social Work Action Network.

Michael Lavalette is Professor of Social Work and Social Policy at Liverpool Hope University and National Co-ordinator of the Social Work Action Network.

Series editors' introduction

For much of its history, mainstream social work in Britain has been a fairly conservative profession. It has often reflected the dominant political ideologies of the day, while presenting itself as resolutely 'non-political'. Thus, the first social work organisation, the Charity Organisation Society (COS) (1869), rigorously adhered to the Poor Law notion that the poor could be divided into 'deserving' and 'undeserving', rejected any form of state intervention aimed at improving people's lives (including free school meals and old-age pensions) and saw the practice of individual casework as the best antidote to the spread of socialist ideas.

By contrast, social work in the 1960s reflected a broad social democratic consensus, evident in the recommendations of the Seebohm Report in England and Wales and the Kilbrandon Report in Scotland on the basis of which the new generic social work departments were established. In most respects, the social work of this period reflected a huge advance on the punitive individualism of the COS (and, it should be said, the punitive individualism of our own time). Even then, however, there was still a tendency to pathologise (albeit it was communities rather than individuals that were seen as failing) and to ignore the extent to which statutory social work intervention continued to be experienced by service users as oppressive and paternalistic. Be that as it may, the progressive possibilities of the new departments were soon cut short by the onset of a global economic crisis in 1973 to which the Labour governments of the time could offer no answer, except cuts and belt-tightening.

What is also true, however, as we have argued elsewhere (Lavalette and Ferguson, 2007), is that there has always been another tradition in social work, an activist/radical approach which has sought to present an alternative vision both to individualism and also to paternalist, top-down collectivism. This approach, which flourished in the UK in the 1970s, located the problems experienced by those who sought social work support in the material conditions of their lives and attempted to develop practice responses that challenged these conditions and their effects.

One source of theory underpinning that approach was the excellent series Critical Texts in Social Work and the Welfare State, edited by Peter Leonard and published by Macmillan.

Three decades on, this current series aims to similarly deepen and refresh the critical and radical social work tradition by providing a range of critical perspectives on key issues in contemporary social work. Social work has always been a contested profession but the need for a space for debate and discussion around ways forward for those committed to a social work practice informed by notions of social justice has never been greater. The issues are complex. How should social workers view personalisation, for example? In an era of austerity, can social work be about more than simply safeguarding and rationing scarce services? Will the integration of services in areas such as mental health lead to improved services or simply greater domination of medical models? Do social work practices offer an escape from managerialism and bureaucracy or are they simply a Trojan horse for privatisation?

These are some of the questions which contributors to this series – academics, practitioners, service users and movement activists – will address. Not all of those contributing to these texts would align themselves with the critical or radical tradition. What they have in common, however, is a commitment to a view of social work which is much wider than the currently dominant neoliberal models and a belief that notions of human rights and social justice should be at the heart of the social work project.

Personalisation: Peter Beresford

Personalisation is one of the central ideas within modern social work – yet it remains deeply controversial. For advocates it is a means of ensuring that service users have a real say in the provision of services that impact on their lives. For critics it is a way of cheapening services and working conditions while tying service users into a culture of consumerism and market forms of care delivery.

Here, Peter Beresford draws together present research on personalisation and argues that it fails to match the aspirations of service users for services geared to meet human need that are atuned to appropriate levels of service user control.

In the commentaries that follow, a range of voices are presented. Some are more supportive of some of the themes of the personalisation agenda, others present the perspectives of social care workers, whilst others offer a service user perspective.

Taken together, this engaging collection will provide a valuable source for practitioners, service users, students and academics trying to make sense of the personalisation agenda and its impact on the lives of service users.

Personalisation: from solution to problem?

Peter Beresford

Introduction

'Personalisation' is without question the dominating idea and development currently in social work and social care. In England, it has had a high profile since the publication of the government's *Putting people first* in 2007 (HM Government, 2007), and the likelihood is that it will remain so in the UK for the foreseeable future. All three mainstream political parties have signed up to the idea of 'personalisation'. It has become an article of faith for the English Department of Health and numerous consultancies and pressure groups work to advance its implementation.

Yet, 'personalisation' is a term that has no clear or agreed meaning and does not have a place in many established dictionaries. Many of its strongest critics have been service users and their organisations, and practitioners and their trade unions, although, ironically, among the major claims made for it are that it will improve service users' lives and restore professional practice to its original progressive value base.

Whatever we may think of 'personalisation', those concerned with social work, social care and health must grapple with it because it is now increasingly shaping both the conceptual frameworks of these fields and their day-to-day professional and occupational practice. So, whether our starting point is as helping professionals, students,

–

managers, educators, researchers, service users or carers, we need to make sense of this development to understand how it may affect us and how we may negotiate and respond to it most helpfully. A key aim of this article is to help readers to do this.

Historical insights

Social work and social care in Britain both have a chequered history. They have been devalued, underfunded, neglected, stigmatised and misunderstood. There has been no golden age for either of them, and the views and experience of service users have often been negative (Harding and Beresford, 1996). 'Personalisation' is far from the first instance of a contentious and ambiguous development emerging in social work and social care. Indeed, their history can be seen to be littered with such innovations. One such development was 'patch'-based or 'community' social work. Interestingly, links are now being made between personalisation and community social work. Personalisation has been compared with community social work and is seen as having the potential to offer the same gains (see: http://www.communitycare.co.uk/blogs/adult-care-blog/2011/08/social-care-dependency-and-the-return-of-community-social-work.html [accessed 1 July 2013]).

Patch/community social work

Patch and community social work are most closely associated with the 1982 Barclay Report (Barclay Committee, 1982; Beresford, 1982). These two overlapping ideas were both based on an emphasis on geographic community and decentralisation. While there was some blurring of the two, a key distinction was that the 'patch' area tended to be constructed as smaller. Both highlighted the importance of being near to local communities, working closely with them and involving them actively. Pioneering examples of such grassroots ways of working were identified and generated much interest from social workers and others who were already disillusioned with the cumbersome and bureaucratic 'social services departments' established in the early 1970s (Hadley and McGrath, 1980). Patch and community social work were sold on:

- challenging and reducing bureaucracy;
- small being beautiful;
- overcoming administrative divisions by having a unified local presence, which was often embodied in a 'patch' or 'neighbourhood office' (in some areas, decentralisation was across the range of local authority services, all to be accessed in a 'one-stop shop'); and
- buildings links and relationships with local people, which helped prevent problems arising and made them part of the community (Hadley and McGrath, 1980; Hadley and Hatch, 1981; Hadley et al, 1984).

Interestingly, patch and community social work, like personalisation, emerged at a time of severe economic recession and major political and ideological change. While the developments that were included under the patch/community social work banner were presented as progressive and innovative, they came to be seen as much more heterogeneous and complex. As time went on, it became clear that patch and community social work had regressive as well as progressive implications and associations. Thus, emerging evidence and discussions highlighted their:

- over-reliance on unrealistic and often excluding notions of geographic community (to the exclusion of other ideas and forms of community);
- reliance on the anti-state rhetoric of the political Right;
- limited evidence base;
- reliance on people doing things for themselves in the name of self-help and mutual aid;
- tendency to transfer responsibility rather than power and control;
- association with cuts in paid staff and the substitution of lower-paid for professional staff;

- increasing emphasis and reliance instead on the unpaid work of women, particularly with the emerging idea of 'informal care' and 'informal carers';
- tendency to misinterpret and appropriate black and minority ethnic community networks;
- difficulties in ensuring a consistent and coherent system of support across localities; and
- association with privatisation (Beresford and Croft, 1984a, 1984b, 1986).

What is perhaps most interesting about patch and community social work is how limited their lives were. Advanced with enthusiasm in the early 1980s, schemes were already being dismantled by the latter part of the decade. East Sussex, a high-profile pioneer of patch-based social work, just as quickly closed its neighbourhood offices and moved back to a traditional system of specialist social work. By the beginning of the 1990s, the government had switched its attention and interest to 'care' or 'case management', which has been the dominant approach to local authority social work, particularly adult social work, up until the introduction of personalisation.

There are some significant lessons to be learned from this history when considering personalisation. First is the ambiguity of patch and community social work. While they gained much support from progressive commentators and practitioners and pioneering examples, like the patch teams in the London Borough of Hammersmith and Fulham, really seemed to break new ground, for example, in relation to the emergence of HIV/AIDS (Beresford and Harding, 1993), strong concerns were also expressed about the negative potential of this social work approach, especially from feminist and radical social work commentators (Finch and Groves, 1980, 1983; Langan and Lee, 1989). Second, patch and community social work offer a powerful reminder of the vulnerability and tenuousness of major changes and innovations in social work and social care, even when they gain high-level political, policy and professional support. Their actual shelf lives were very short and they seem to have left little legacy, except perhaps in the consciousness of those practitioners and service users who valued and benefitted from them. We will do well to remember both these points as we turn to personalisation in order to minimise the risk of repeating past mistakes.

The emergence of personalisation

SLK Training and Consultancy, one of many such consultancies set up in the wake of the government's commitment to roll out personalisation, offers a helpful face-value definition of the term, which reflects much of the conventional wisdom and prevailing thinking about it:

> Personalisation, often referred to as the complete transformation of adult social care, also means making universal services such as transport, housing and education accessible to all citizens. Personalisation is about putting individuals firmly in the driving seat of building a system of care and support that is designed with their full involvement and tailored to meet their own unique needs. This is a completely different approach to an historic 'one size fits all' system of individuals having to access, and fit into, care and support services that already exist which have been designed and commissioned on their behalf by Local Authorities for example. Individuals will receive their own budget and can decide how, who with and where they wish to spend that budget in order to meet their needs and achieve their desired outcomes. Whilst there is initial focus on social care and support services, the principles of personalisation are being embedded into a range of other public service areas such as health and education. (From: www.slk-consultancy.org.uk/ viewnews.php?id=34 [accessed 1 September 2011])

As this statement suggests, the term 'personalisation' was originally used to describe people accessing a cash budget (personal or individual budget) to spend on their support, to put together what help and services they wanted. However, more recently, there has been a shift in the term's official usage. It is now also used by the government to mean people having more choice and control and a more customised service, regardless of what service or form of support they receive and however it is provided. No clear reason has been offered for this change, although it does, of course, result in a much vaguer definition. At the same time, official measures of progress towards the 'transformation' of social care have still tended to be presented in terms of the numbers and proportion of service users who have moved to personal budgets. Thus, personalisation is still closely, but not solely, associated with budgets, although there is now some ambiguity about the idea.

The presentation of personalisation

Personalisation in social care represents a major shift in public policy, with strong ministerial support, the allocation of more than £500 million by government to take it forward – an unusually large amount in the usually cash-strapped field of social care – and an official emphasis on its radical structural and transformative nature (Boxall et al, 2009). Yet, despite the scale of the change, it was publicly presented and significantly constructed in terms of a number of personal stories. These were stories of service users who were beneficiaries of the new arrangements for support through personal budgets. Often, new policies or initiatives are presented in terms of particular pioneering examples (as happened, for instance, with patch) or through spotlighting specific programmes or innovating organisations. Certainly, with personalisation and personal budgets, some particular local authorities, like Essex and Oldham, have also been highlighted.

However, in the case of personalisation, the story was primarily told through a series of personal stories. A significant exception has been the helpful resources produced by the Social Care Institute for Excellence (eg Carr, 2010a, 2010b). These high-profile and frequently repeated stories featured regularly in the media and at conferences and were cited by policymakers and politicians. Notable examples include those of personal budget users Gavin Croft and Julia Winter. As these were reported:

–

6

Gavin Croft … spent £375 of care money from Oldham council on a season ticket for Rochdale FC for a fellow fan to accompany him to home matches and commentate on the action on the pitch. Croft, who suffers from multiple sclerosis and whose vision is impaired by a degenerative condition, recruited his companion from the supporters' internet site. Croft's wife said that allowing her husband to spend his care money in this way gave her a much-needed break. 'It has been great. It gives me the only time I get off all week and I don't have to watch football in the wet and the cold,' she told the *Manchester Evening News*. Croft said he also enjoyed going to the pub after the match with his Saturday afternoon 'carer'….

In Essex, for example, a personal budget-holder [Julia Winter] with serious respiratory problems that kept her in hospital for three months a year, had air conditioning installed in her house – an adaptation that neither direct payments not traditional services would have paid for. As a result, she has not been back to hospital, making savings to social care and the NHS. (From: http://www. guardian.co.uk/society/2008/jul/02/longtermcare.socialcare2 [accessed 15 June 2013])

The thrust of such stories tended to be the same; framed in human, flesh-and-blood terms, they made clear that:

- personal budgets could make life better for people;
- they could reduce their need to use formal services;
- they were superior to traditional arrangements – even more recent ones, like direct payments;
- they helped save money; and
- they made it possible for everyone to be a winner – the service user, their family, service providers and the tax-payer (Leadbeater, 2008).

Significantly, a relatively narrow range of such stories tended to be highlighted. The service users concerned (like the two mentioned earlier) were sometimes actively and closely involved with the new development, linked with authorities and organisations that were taking it forward. However, while service users were at the centre of the selling of personal budgets and the initiative was powerfully fronted by them, significantly, this was not a user-led development. The organisations most closely associated with its development – In Control, Mencap, the Department of Health Care Services Improvement Partnership (CSIP) and particular local authorities – were either conventional voluntary/third sector or state-related organisations and key instigators and advocates of the development tended to be non-service users, again, with histories in conventional state and charitable organisations, and in managerial and professional roles.

This might not seem a powerful body of evidence for such a massive change in policy. However, governments, which repeatedly stressed the importance of evidence-based policy and practice, did not seem to be deterred by this. Indeed, the move to personal budgets and personalisation has generally not been one based on messages from evidence.

The evidence base

The government embarked upon a policy of personalisation without having any strong evidence to support it (Boxall et al, 2009). What evidence there was mostly came from the organisations advocating this shift in policy, like In Control (Leadbeater, 2004; Poll et al, 2006; Waters and Duffy, 2007; Hatton et al, 2008). The government made the policy move and large-scale associated investment even before it had the results of its own research. By the time the evidence from this project (the IBSEN [Individual Budgets Evaluation Network] project) was available – and it was qualified by the late start of the pilot projects upon which it was based – the government had already committed itself to massive policy change.

The findings from the IBSEN project were complex and qualified. At this time, political interest was in 'individual' budgets, where the aim was to combine a range of funding streams and not only the 'personal' budgets tied to social care. The study identified:

- problems in unifying such different funding streams – for which much had been claimed for individual budgets;
- no clear savings generally from individual budgets; and
- significant differences in the apparent effectiveness and suitability of individual budgets for different groups, for example, with a positive response from mental health service users, but major problems identified in relation to older people (the largest group of adult social care service users) and people with multiple and complex impairments.

Problems with personal budgets in relation to people with multiple and complex impairments were further evidenced by a review undertaken for the Commission for Social Care Inspection (Henwood and Hudson, 2009).

The emerging evidence

Thus, on the evidence, there was little justification for the massive switch made to personal budgets. From a relatively small number of pilot projects, the government moved to roll out personal budgets and personalisation as the default system of delivering social care support. There were dissenting organisations and voices – people who raised concerns about the speed and nature of the move and its lack of underpinning evidence. This author was one of them (Beresford, 2007, 2008a). Notable among these voices were those of service users and practitioners who were not part of the project but could expect to be signed up to it. Such voices and such cautions were not encouraged. There is no doubt that such perspectives were often not welcome in policy forums, on conference platforms and in contributing to the literature and discussion. I can say this as one such voice, from my own experience and witnessing others.

However, as evidence has emerged and been consolidated, it has confirmed the concerns that were being raised as the government rushed to implement social care 'transformation' within its self-set and unprecedented timetable of three years. There is now evidence from local and national studies, service users, practitioners, trade unionists, and independent researchers. Now, a very different story is emerging from that which we were originally told.

An early warning was offered by participants in a one-day conference organised by the London Self-Directed Support Forum in 2009. Delegates and speakers represented many different points of view and a wide range of constituencies involved in and affected by personalisation and personal budgets, including support staff (in-house and from the voluntary sector), user-controlled organisations, consultants working in the field, carers and family members, advocates, welfare advisers, and others. Key problems they identified with personal budgets were:

- Uncertainty – was there real political commitment to transforming social care?
- A difficult context – a time of increasing need and diminishing access to support.
- Inadequate funding – increasing rationing, with not enough money locally and nationally.
- Questions about who is in control – fears that service users and their user-controlled organisations were not really in control of this development.
- The limits of consumerism – concerns that the individualised 'customer' is far from being 'king' in the new arrangements (Beresford, 2009a).

Headlines from a 2011 national *Community Care*/UNISON national survey of personal budgets added to such concerns, indicating that:

- 83% of practitioners surveyed said that cuts to adult care budgets in their areas would impede the operation of personal budgets;

- almost half (48%) thought that personal budgets were not of sufficient value to help users meet their needs;
- 37% disagreed that the resource allocation system in their area effectively allocated money to people in line with their needs – 47% agreed;
- 33% said that resources had been the greatest barrier in making progress with implementing personalisation;
- 57% said that users did not have a genuine choice of services from the social care market, and evidence that personal budgets were not changing the services that people received; and
- 44% of respondents said that people were generally buying the same kinds of support under personal budgets as under traditionally commissioned packages of care – just 3% said that most people in their areas were buying different kinds of support with personal budgets than before.

Now, only a minority of social workers believe that personal budgets benefit services users in the medium to long term (see: http://www.communitycare.co.uk/Articles/2011/05/25/116868/social-workers-losing-faith-in-personalisation.htm [accessed 30 June 2013]). A similar picture was provided by a further *Community Care* survey carried out in 2013, highlighting inadequate support, lack of control by service users and their families, and increasing bureaucracy (see: http://www.communitycare.co.uk/state-of-personalisation-2013/ [accessed 30 June 2013]).

Two major studies in mid-2011 – an Association of Directors of Adult Social Services (ADASS) survey of progress on personalisation and the Personal Budgets Outcome Evaluation Tool (POET) survey – both highlighted problems and a lack of progress. ADASS found that while 'personal budget numbers in England doubled from April 2010 to March 2011, to almost 340,000 – 35% of eligible users and carers – nearly all of the 2010/11 increase came in the form of council-managed budgets'. According to *Community Care*, the POET survey found that 'service users on direct payments they managed themselves "reported significantly more positive outcomes than people receiving council-managed budgets"'; 'The Adass findings sparked concerns that some councils were allocating people nominal personal budgets without offering them choice and control' (from: http://www.communitycare. co.uk/Articles/22/06/2011/117050/direct-payments-stall-despite-evidence-of-better-outcomes.htm [accessed 26 September 2011]).

The POET national personal budget survey carried out in 2011 by In Control, the organisation most closely associated with the advancement of personal budgets, reported positive results (http://www.in-control. org.uk/4466.aspx [accessed 3 September 2011]), but also, according to David Brindle of *The Guardian*, 'adds the critical rider that personal budgets work well for everyone when they get full support to maximise the advantages. Short of that, the idea can be tarnished'. Furthermore, he cited Rob Greenland of Social Business Brokers, who said: 'People are starting to publicly acknowledge that we are struggling to make personal budgets work'.

Brindle also quoted the ADASS as admitting:

> that only one in three budgets is given in the form of a direct payment. Most people are told how much they are entitled to, but never get to handle the money. 'Nearly all the increase has been in "managed" personal budgets, with no significant increase in direct payment numbers in the last year,' the association says. (Brindle, 2011, p 4)

The methodological limitations of a follow-up POET survey, reporting in 2013, unfortunately also undermine its value as a source of further evidence in support of personal budgets policy (see Slasberg et al, forthcoming[a]; forthcoming[b]).

The Demos Personal Budget Market Intelligence project, operating since 2009, additionally casts light on the barriers facing government aspirations. From a sample in 10 local authorities:

- two thirds had never heard of personal budgets;
- only 5% said that they would change their existing care package if they had a personal budget;

- a strong divide in preferences emerged, indicating that it would be necessary to maintain existing services for half of service users as well as developing alternatives for the rest; and
- 75% of people said that they would need some help to maintain personal budgets (Claudia Wood, Demos, personal communication, Enrych Conference, Birmingham, 21 September 2011).

A 2011 National Audit Office (NAO) report on personal budgets concluded that 'shortcomings must be addressed if value for money is to be secured in the future for users of social care "personal budgets" once they are extended to all eligible users by April 2013' (from: http://www.nao.org.uk/publications/press_notice_home/1012/10121458.aspx [accessed 26 September 2011]). Issues that the report highlighted included that:

- more needs to be done to ensure that care markets deliver a genuine choice of services to all users;
- support should be available to help them exercise choice;
- essential services relied on by vulnerable people continue to be provided in the event of the failure of a major provider;
- the overall impact on cost has not been evaluated; and
- while there are examples of good practice in some local authorities, such as offering help to those with personal budgets to plan their care, these are very localised (NAO, 2011).

A 2011 survey of personal budget practitioners by the London Self-Directed Support Forum provided findings from front-line workers. While some positive developments were reported, most practitioners said that both they and service users did not understand self-directed support. Most did not think that new systems of assessment ensured more choice and control and that people were offered independent support to complete self-assessment forms. Most did not understand the 'resource allocation system' (RAS), which was meant to be personal budgets' unique selling point. In a majority of cases, the RAS seemed neither to be matching need nor coming closer to ensuring adequate financial resources. It had mostly tended to *reduce* people's budgets. In most settings, there were still restrictions on what people could purchase with their personal budget – which flew in the face of the essential point of moving to personal budgets. For a sizable minority of people, there were still no annual reviews, and as for the government's demand that the system should be outcome-based, an outcome-based review process was still not in place for around half of cases (Beresford, 2011a).

Not all was doom and gloom however. In a number of cases, we were seeing more creative support plans, a clear definition of a service brokerage scheme and support plans getting the go-ahead. In about half of cases, the brokerage service was properly separate from support planning. In most cases, there was ongoing support. But this is hardly the kind of transformation we were promised and it is clear that we are still far from the 'transparent' and 'de-bureaucratised' system of customised support that disabled people and other social care service users were promised. Perhaps most worrying, at least half of the participants in this survey thought that personalisation was a tick-box exercise – which did not make for meaningful improvement (Beresford, 2011a).

So, if we now try to sum up, putting together independent evidence that has become available about personal budgets, as well as the accounts of service users, carers and practitioners emerging from their own informal discussions, the picture that emerges is one of:

- a frequently heavily bureaucratic RAS;
- reducing eligibility in a time of severe cuts;
- reduced personal budgets;
- cash sums top-sliced for administration;
- service users without adequate support to manage schemes, narrowing the range of people able to access and maintain them (eg in relation to personal and family situation, health status, class, age, ethnicity, education, confidence, and cognitive ability);
- some local authorities simply treating the move to personal budgets as a numbers game, rebadging the same old service arrangements in cash terms as if it meant anything different; and

—

- a postcode lottery of how transformation is actually implemented, with some localities making real attempts to improve and change and others acting as if they hoped that if they did nothing, it would all eventually go away.

Selling individual/personal budgets

Given the original lack of supportive evidence accompanying them, the cautions expressed at the time and the discouraging pattern of emerging evidence, we might wonder why personal/individual budgets were taken up so enthusiastically by politicians and policymakers in England. The answer seems to lie in how they were sold. Their advocates made the simple and bold case that they could offer better for less. One of their most prominent theoreticians, Charles Leadbeater of the think tank Demos, repeatedly claimed that they would save money. In 2008, Leadbeater suggested that savings 'could be as high as 45%' (Leadbeater, 2008; Leadbeater et al, 2008). The promise of financial savings always appeals to politicians, and in relation to a service like social care, which has long been underfunded and strapped for cash, this appeal was visible and powerful. Speakers on major public platforms, politicians and policymakers constantly repeated the mantra that individual/personal budgets offered a route to better services and support for less money, cutting unnecessary bureaucracy. Significantly, exactly the same claims were previously made by some of its key advocates for patch and community social work.

There was never any evidence to support this claim for individual/personal budgets and while there can be no doubt that a good-quality system of 'self-directed support' based on direct payments can offer service users good support, it has never been demonstrated that this is a cheaper option. Indeed, for obvious reasons, it may cost more than traditional inadequately funded arrangements for providing social care support. A generation earlier, the same claims of better for less and reduced bureaucracy were made for patch and community social work by some of its advocates, again, frequently framed in terms of achieving the former through ensuring the latter. Similarly, these were never evidenced.

The background to personalisation

So far in this article, we have looked at the idea of personalisation in relation to patch and community social work, seen its rapid rise and limited evidence base, and examined its historic association with individual and personal budgets. However, this only takes us some of the way to understanding personalisation and gaining an explanation for the significant status it has gained. To achieve a fuller understanding, we need to look more closely at both its background and its conceptualisation.

Individual and personal budgets were advanced in the noughties as a brave new idea. Simon Duffy, founder of In Control, a key organisation in the development of individual/personal budgets, was awarded the prestigious gold 'Albert Medal' by the Royal Society of Arts for his work in developing 'self-directed support' based on individual/personal budgets. He has been identified as 'the man leading a revolution in social care' (from: http://www.centreforwelfarereform.org/who-we-are/team/simon-duffy.html [accessed 30 June 2013]). However, the reality is that individual/personal budgets were derived from the direct payments inspired and developed by the disabled people's movement almost a generation ago.

Disabled people's direct payments

The disabled people's movement, developing in the UK from the late 1960s, rejected the paternalism of state welfare policies. However, it was also critical of both the market and charitable sector as similarly rooted in medicalised individual understandings of disability, which it saw as casting disabled people as the cause of their own problems and dependence. Members of the movement saw the 'tragedy' model of disability, which they felt that existing services perpetuated, as discriminating against people with impairments, marginalising, impoverishing and excluding them.

The disabled people's movement developed a new social model of disability that distinguished between people's perceived physical, sensory and intellectual impairments and the negative social reaction to them, which they described as disability. From this flowed the philosophy of independent living and an associated movement that spread rapidly through North America to the UK and Europe from California. The key principle of independent living was that disabled people and other service users should have the support and access to mainstream opportunities needed to live their lives on as equal terms as possible as non-disabled people (UPIAS/Disability Alliance, 1975; Oliver and Barnes, 1998).

Direct payments were a groundbreaking development rooted in this pioneering philosophy, values and theory. Their essential aim was to put disabled people and then other service users in control of their support as part of a broader independent living approach, which would also work for full and equal inclusion, access and participation in mainstream life and services to enable them to live on as equal terms as possible as non-disabled people and non-service users. Direct payments were conceived of as representing a sum of money under the control of service users. Thus, from the start, they were rooted in a set of clear yardsticks:

- The service user would be in control of their support.
- The amount of money provided would match the needs that they had in order to secure their equal human and civil rights.
- They would have the support they needed to be able to manage a direct payments system – to be provided through the development of a network of local user-led organisations (ULOs) or disabled people's organisations (DPOs).

Such organisations would not only provide the infrastructure to support people to operate such direct payments schemes, but also be a valued source of collective services and good-quality personal assistants to provide appropriate support. We know from a large body of evidence that direct payments provided unprecedented opportunities for disabled people and other service users to gain greater control over their lives, increase their life chances and even improve their health and well-being.

Yet, while introduced by new legislation in the 1990s, with pioneering initiatives going back 20 years earlier, progress was slow, particularly so in some areas. There was little determined pressure from the centre to overcome such inertia and resistance. Only a tiny proportion of service users were enabled to access direct payments. They were run by local authorities and critics felt that these often did not understand direct payments and bureaucratised and over-controlled them, with funding levels set in line with budgetary restrictions rather than to meet service users' rights and needs (Oliver and Barnes, 1998; Stainton and Boyce, 2004; Riddell et al, 2005).

The new interest in personal budgets

The new interest in individual and personal budgets emerging in recent years has been different in both its origins and the response it has inspired to that of disabled people. The impetus was very different:

- it came from non-disabled people and from non-user-controlled organisations;
- it was disassociated from all the key criteria established by disabled people and detailed earlier;
- there was no commitment that disabled people/service users should be in control of the development – in general terms or as an individual recipient of a personal budget;
- service users/disabled people would certainly not necessarily be ensured any support to run such schemes;
- it was slow to address issues of diversity and inclusion; and
- the amount of money provided for a budget was not linked to any criteria of independent living, but rather simply a reallocation of existing generally inadequate funding within arbitrary and unhelpful eligibility criteria and means testing (Boxall et al, 2009).

These two developments can be seen to have significantly different ideological underpinnings. The first was based on the democratising impulse of the collective organisations of disabled people's and service users' movements, with a commitment to user control, involvement and empowerment. The second appears to have been more closely bound up with broader managerialist/consumerist agendas of government public policy and services. While direct payments were originally argued for by the liberatory or new social movements of service users as an expression of collective action, individual and personal budgets have been more closely linked with state and third sector models based on 'professional expertise' and market-driven provision. Different actors have initiated developments for self-directed support in potentially different directions, based on possibly competing philosophies. The shift from the original direct payments to personal budgets reflects a move from a means of empowerment to an underfunded market-based voucher system. From a replacement for a traditional and inadequate set of services, we have moved to an exchange relationship, which casts the service user as a consumer rather than citizen with rights – to a model that is market-based and market-driven rather than liberatory in intent (Ferguson, 2007; Beresford, 2008b; Roulstone and Morgan, 2009). Of course, personal budgets may still benefit some service users. This would not be difficult, sadly, given the poor quality of much traditional social care provision. But that is not what was promised with the move to personalisation. We were promised something much better for all and that is not what is happening and there is no evidence that it is likely to, especially when the existing approach chimes so well with the cutting, privatising and individualising approach to social care that has, in recent years, to different degrees, gained major cross-party political support.

To take stock, what emerges from an examination of history here is that direct payments and personal budgets can serve very different purposes, are highly ambiguous and may be associated with fundamentally different ideologies. While individual and personal budgets have been presented by their advocates as offering increased choice and control to service users, what becomes clear is that they are actually just a delivery system with regressive as well as progressive potential. As we are currently seeing, they may be used to increase or improve the support available to service users, or indeed actually to reduce or adversely affect it. This connects with another key problem that has helped create confusion in this field. It has not been clear whether personalisation is a means or an end. Is it a way of achieving objectives, or does it inherently embrace certain objectives? There has been a continuing lack of clarity about this, not least because, as we have seen, while the term was originally presented as if synonymous with personal budgets, more recently, it has been used by the government to signal a broader concern with choice and control across all kinds of services and methods of delivering support.

This leads to the second big issue identified here: what does personalisation actually mean? The term – a jargon word that conveys little meaning to outsiders – has been poorly defined. Its definition has mainly sprung from the government and policymakers, with little broader consensus or shared understanding.

Making sense of personalisation

The four-year 'Standards We Expect' national research and development project, supported by the Joseph Rowntree Foundation, offers some helpful insights here. One of the underpinning aims of this independent project was to try to gain a better understanding of personalisation (Beresford et al, 2011).

The purpose of the project was to find out what people at the front line of social care – service users, carers, face-to-face practitioners and managers – saw personalisation or person-centred support as meaning. Instead of creating additional external definitions, it aimed to find out what it meant to the key groups most closely involved in it. The term 'person-centred support' rather than 'personalisation' was used because of the latter's jargonistic nature. The project was also concerned with finding out what these groups saw as the barriers in the way of personalisation and how these could be overcome. There was considerable consensus among service users, carers and face-to-face practitioners over all these issues.

They did not associate person-centred support narrowly with personal or individual budgets. Instead, participants' definition of person-centred support was strongly based on values rather than techniques or procedures. They saw person-centred support as an approach to support that was strongly value-based, where the relationship between service user and worker was of central importance.

Key components that they cited were:

- putting the person at the centre, rather than fitting them into services;
- treating service users as individuals;
- ensuring choice and control for service users;
- setting goals with them for support;
- emphasising the importance of the relationship between service users and practitioners;
- listening to service users and acting on what they say;
- providing up-to-date, accessible information about appropriate services;
- flexibility; and
- a positive approach, which highlights what service users might be able to do, not what they cannot do (Beresford et al, 2011, pp 39–62).

They talked about person-centred support in terms of seeing people as individuals and organising services and support around them, rather than vice versa – 'treating people how you would want to be treated', so that 'the power is with the person, not the organisation' (Beresford et al, 2011). Their understanding of person-centred support can be seen as a reaction against long-standing paternalistic and institutionalising approaches to support and social care. They offered a coherent picture of what person-centred support or personalisation should mean.

Barriers in the way of personalisation

As has been seen, individual and personal budgets were originally presented by their advocates as a radical solution to the problems that have long beset social care. The message was that making the move to implement them wholesale had the potential to transform social care and this was the policy that the government adopted. However, participants in the 'Standards We Expect' project highlighted a wide range of barriers that they felt had to be addressed before personalisation/person-centred support could be achieved routinely and for all. Not only was each of these barriers seen to create its own obstacles inhibiting such an approach, but, combined, they magnified such difficulties.

Thus, if the claim made for individual and personal budgets was that they could transform the social care system, what service users, carers, practitioners and managers emphasised was that major changes were needed in the *overall system* if it was to deliver what they understood by personalisation/person-centred support. Key barriers they identified included:

- The lack of a well-supported, skilled and well-trained workforce and low levels of staffing. Generally, poor terms and conditions were associated with low retention and high turnover rates, offering little prospect of ensuring an adequate workforce to match predictions of greatly increasing demand.
- Increasing reliance being placed on family members as 'informal carers'. Without sufficient support for carers themselves or help for them to facilitate service users' independence, this provides an inadequate and inappropriate basis for meeting increased future need.
- Restrictions on the lives of many long-term and residential service users by continuing institutionalisation. This disempowers them, undermines their confidence, limits their potential and prevents them gaining the skills to live fuller, more equal lives.

- Organisational barriers to person-centred support. These operate at all levels. Participants cite increased bureaucratisation, tightening administrative controls, inflexible organisations, crude target setting and an emphasis on 'negative risk', often framed in terms of health and safety requirements.
- Social care practice. Participants saw this as following from a disempowering service culture that is still often paternalistic and inflexible – 'making unhelpful assumptions about what service users can and can't do', as one said – and restricting the crucial relationship between them and practitioners.
- Service users' restricted access to mainstream policies and services, keeping them within social care services and undermining the holistic approach of person-centred support to live on as equal and inclusive terms as is possible. Three particular areas mentioned were: travel and transport, education, and continuing disability discrimination. People living in rural areas and from black and minority ethnic communities face additional barriers.
- Barriers relating to service users' circumstances and experience. Many lack the support they need to be able to access and take advantage of person-centred support. There is a lack of capacity-building through ensuring accessible information, advice, guidance and advocacy (Beresford, 2011b).

The 'Standards We Expect' project found that much was being done in local services to deal with these barriers. Some services, managers and practitioners, linking with service users and carers, were working hard to overcome them. However, such efforts to challenge barriers at the local level were not enough to make it possible for person-centred support to become the norm for most users. Such barriers seem to be rooted in two larger and interrelated problems: the chronic inadequacy of social care funding; and the continued existence of a social care culture at odds with person-centred support. This problematic culture was reflected in continuing institutionalisation, control, paternalism and inflexibility in services, and reliance on a 'deficit' model rather than on the philosophy of independent living as the basis for providing support. Funding problems also seemed to lie at the heart of workforce inadequacies, over-reliance on unpaid carers, insufficient and inaccessible mainstream services, and lack of suitable advocacy, advice and information services (Beresford et al, 2011).

Conclusion

A 2011 text on personal budgets was framed in terms of 'understanding the personalisation narrative' (Needham, 2011b). It referred to advocates of personalisation and those who have 'problematised it' (this author is placed in the latter category). How far we have come from the liberatory concerns of the disabled people's movement in their development of direct payments is highlighted by a concluding comment: 'it is hard not to feel some sympathy for campaigners from disability organisations who are encountering the same set of critiques that sought to slow down the implementation of direct payments 20 years ago' (Needham, 2011b, p 170).

The reality, of course, is that it is campaigners from the disabled people's movement, among others, who have been 'problematising' moves to personal budgets as individualising and consumerist and that their critiques are far from being based on the traditional objections raised against direct payments. Debate about personal budgets has certainly been polarised. Key advocates like Routledge, Duffy and Leadbeater have all been closely involved in policy development, sometimes with the government itself. All this again highlights the ambiguity of personal budgets as part of public policy and also the subtlety, complexity and ahistorical nature of much discourse that has developed around them.

Personalisation in social care has a remarkably short history for a major public policy reform (Samuel, 2008). From the start to the present is but a few years. Yet, much has happened and much has changed in that time. From being seen as the solution to the major problems facing social care, it is now seen as itself in question (see: http://www.guardian.co.uk/society/joepublic/2011/aug/15/direct-payments-care [accessed 12 September 2011]; http://www.communitycare.co.uk/

blogs/adult-care-blog/2011/09/the-personalisation-dream-is-dying. html [accessed 1 July 2013]). Personalisation has moved from being presented as a radical solution through the large-scale implementation of individual and personal budgets, to rising recognition of the need for there to be a wide range of changes in social care if it is to achieve personalisation (Martin Routledge, plenary speaker, national *Community Care* Personalisation Conference, 30 April 2008). Personal budgets have increasingly emerged as ambiguous. They can be part of a movement for liberation, as the direct payments originally developed by the disabled people's movement were envisaged, or part of a market-centred move to cut costs, privatise provision and rely on unpaid caring, as governments more recently seem to have conceived of them.

In some authorities, personal budgets have been used to mean little more than a rebranding of existing and traditional arrangements. In others, they have provided the opportunity to extend access to direct payments to more and a wider range of service users. In some cases, and in some areas, moves to personal budgets and personalisation have meant the loss of access to traditional collective services (without replacement), having to pay for them or having to take on all the responsibilities and risks of running a personal budget without adequate information, back-up or support. However, some service users, particularly where a ULO is involved in providing infrastructural support, are fortunate enough to have in place a support system that corresponds to the liberatory ideal originally envisaged by disabled pioneers of the independent living movement. Meanwhile, practitioners, carers and service users must try to make the most of the system that has been implemented.

What is difficult to predict is what the future holds for personalisation. Is it likely as a policy to be progressive or regressive in its effect? At a time of massive cuts in public services, including social care, it is difficult to be optimistic. The context is one of reductions in the number of social workers and support services and narrowing eligibility criteria with stricter needs testing. At present, there seems little likelihood of the essential culture change and sustainable funding required in social care being put in place. With the latest embodiment of personalisation

– the 'Think Local Act Personal' partnership, now located at arm's length from government, with very limited funding – the momentum of the policy also seems to be weakening. The possibility now emerges of 'personalisation' becoming another lost idea, like community social work and patch before it. If this is to be avoided, then it is likely that its main champions, service users, carers and face-to-face practitioners will have a long and vital fight on their hands.

At the same time, where else is there for social care to go other than towards person-centred support and true personalisation? There is no golden age to retreat to, no preferable alternative. It is now clear that personal budgets and personalisation offer no short cut or magic bullet, as their first proponents promised. With rising numbers of disabled people of working age and older and very old people, without radical reform, the likelihood is of ever-less people being able to access support, increasing institutionalisation and reducing quality of life and care. The only way forward is to work for the implementation of true person-centred support. We already know that this is likely to command strong support from the people who are really key to the issue: service users, carers and the practitioners working with them.

Personalisation, participation and policy construction: a critique of influences and understandings

Sarah Carr

When it first appeared, the adult social care personalisation policy seemed to assume that there was a universal understanding of the policy terminology, meaning and aims, which included a rhetorical commitment to 'empowerment', 'co-production' and 'choice and control' (HM Government, 2007). However, Beresford's analysis provides insight into some of the confusions of meaning and contradictions inherent in this policy for adult social care. Other critics and observers also agree that as a public policy discourse, personalisation is imprecise, ambiguous and contains certain internal inconsistencies and tensions (Cutler et al, 2007; Pykett, 2009; Roulstone and Morgan, 2009; Needham, 2011a; 2011b), particularly as regards the conceptualisation, design and operation of the personal budget scheme in England (Boxall et al, 2009; Audit Commission, 2010; Carr, 2011a). This response is an attempt to deepen Beresford's criticisms about personalisation not being 'a user-led development' and offers an expansion of his exploration of its origins by further critiquing the influential ideas of Charles Leadbeater.

Before it was introduced for adult social care, the personalisation agenda had already formed part of the policy for education reform and was being championed by the social policy think tank Demos (for an extensive critique, see Pykett, 2009), particularly through the work of Charles Leadbeater, a former *Financial Times* editor, management consultant and policy advisor to Tony Blair, with no experience in adult social care. Despite this, Leadbeater and Demos had a profound influence on the personalisation agenda for adult social care, with Demos publishing *Making it personal* (Leadbeater et al, 2008), a largely theoretical outline for reform, two months after the 2008 local authority circular outlining the adult social care transformation plans (Department of Health, 2008). Leadbeater et al's report focused on self-directed support and personal budgets. Demos positioned the 'new operating system' of the In Control programme (led by Simon Duffy) as the model for adult social care reform, using evidence from the small-scale evaluation of the first pilot phase focusing on people with learning disabilities in seven local authorities and highlighting particular individual stories to illustrate the positive impact of the 'radical' new approach.

Leadbeater et al argued that 'personal budgets promote choice and will expand the competitive market for social care services, from which budget holders can choose' (Leadbeater et al, 2008, p 47). The Demos colleagues went on to claim that 'in self directed services people have real choice over the services they get but they are not just consumers' (Leadbeater et al, 2008, p 81), but citizens with rights and entitlements who make choices about their lives, and have a collective social dimension beyond individual purchasing activity. This model of 'citizen-consumer' was originally developed by Leadbeater in a series of articles on public sector reform published in *Marxism Today* in the late 1980s and early 1990s, where he conceived of 'progressive individualism' (Leadbeater, 1988) and 'the social market' (Leadbeater, 1991a), and set out a 'manifesto for the public sector' (Leadbeater, 1991b). The theories from these early works, such as 'individually-based collectivism', 'a decentralisation and democratisation of the state' (Leadbeater, 1988, p 18) and 'citizen-led services', appear in the policy construction of personalisation in his Demos policy manifesto-style reports *Personalisation through participation: a new script for public services* (Leadbeater, 2004) and *Personalisation and participation: the future of social care in Scotland* (Leadbeater and Lownsbrough, 2005), and finally in *Making it personal* (Leadbeater et al, 2008). However, his undifferentiated model of citizenship does not necessarily fit with the citizen identities and experiences of people who use social care and mental health services (Rose et al, 2002; Morris, 2005; Rummery, 2006; Ferguson, 2007; Beresford, 2009a), rendering implementation of the adult social care reform policy influenced by Leadbeater's thinking problematic.

References to the origins of direct payments, the social model of disability, the values of the independent living movement, the mental health service user/survivor perspective, the role of social work and the effects of discrimination and social and economic deprivation do not feature in Leadbeater's concept of personalisation for adult social care. This led some social work academics to be very critical of this conceptualisation early on, with Ferguson (2007), in particular, noting that for reasons of inequality and deprivation, many people who use social care services will not fit the model of active citizenship required to benefit from Leadbeater's conception of personal budgets: 'The central issue for Leadbeater is lifestyle change, with health and economic inequalities barely discussed ... the failure to engage with the structural inequalities also vitiates Leadbeater's conception of people who use services' (Ferguson, 2007, p 395). Critics of personalisation point to the fundamental lack of service user involvement and evidence in the construction of policy, the particular model of citizenship used, its internal ideological conflicts, the claims about cost savings, and the speed of its implementation (Beresford, 2009b; Boxall et al, 2009; Carr, 2011b). The public sector union UNISON later voiced workforce concerns about social care funding, pay and conditions, and the increased marketisation associated with personalisation (Land and Himmelweit, 2010).

The *Putting people first* concordat, which officially introduced personalisation, claims that the agenda is about putting 'citizens at the heart of a reformed system' (HM Government, 2007, p 1) and maintains that 'real change will only be achieved through the participation of users and carers at every stage' (HM Government, 2007, p 2). However, it can be argued that one of the key challenges

29

for implementing personalisation in adult social care stems precisely from the fact that the policy and Leadbeater's underpinning theories themselves were constructed *without* the participation of service users and carers. Even in his most radical conception of personalisation, Leadbeater preserves the power of the 'professional' (although it is not clear whether this means the front-line practitioner) in making macro-scale decisions about public service reform: 'the professionals are designing environments, networks and platforms through which people can together devise their own solutions' (Leadbeater, 2004, p 24). So, it appears that one of the most politically influential explanations of personalisation explicitly maintained established, systemic power relations and excluded service users and carers from participating in policy construction at the highest strategic level.

Because service users and carers were excluded from directly contributing to the original policy problem formulation, they could not influence the proposed solutions. Nonetheless, they have been asked to participate in the implementation of those solutions, the main one being personal budgets (Beresford, 2009a, 2009b; Boxall et al, 2009). Instead, those defining how the personalisation policy should work for adult social care borrowed direct payments from the service user movement, but the origins were unacknowledged and direct payments were removed from their specific value base (the social model of disability and independent living [UPIAS, 1975]) and political context to become a universal personalisation mechanism in the form of personal budgets (Beresford, 2009b; Boxall et al, 2009). As noted, service user experiential knowledge, evidence and theories did not appear to inform Leadbeater's original conceptualisation of the free, active and enterprising 'citizen-consumer', whose purchasing power would eventually have a positive effect on public service provision in a 'bottom-up' approach to adult social care 'transformation' in the context of decentralisation and marketisation (Leadbeater, 1988, 1991a, 1991b, 2004; Ferguson, 2007; Scourfield, 2007; Leadbeater et al, 2008). It is here that another of Leadbeater's social theories comes into play: the 'social entrepreneur' (Leadbeater, 1997). These conceptual figures were framed in the Demos report *The rise of the social entrepreneur*

(Leadbeater, 1997) as being the innovators who can eventually achieve reform of the welfare system (it is interesting to note that Leadbeater's examples of innovation do not include Centres for Independent Living or other user- or carer-led initiatives). Critics have pointed out that personalisation reforms such as personal budgets have been strongly shaped by the expectation that the service user should become a 'social entrepreneur':

> This transformation is not simply about the reconstruction of citizens as consumers but the transformation of citizens into both managers and entrepreneurs. New Labour's perspective on citizenship appears to focus less on what the citizen should expect from the state in terms of social rights, and more on how the citizen should be – in this case, active, responsible and enterprising. (Scourfield, 2007, p 112)

There is a fundamental problem with applying Leadbeater's general theories of public sector reform through 'consumer-citizenship' and 'social entrepreneurship' to adult social care: the relationship of citizens who use social care services is not the same as that of non-service user or non-disabled citizens to public or civic services like parks or libraries. Some service user experiences of restrictive or oppressive adult social care and mental health systems and administrative processes (such as assessment) would stand in direct contradiction to Leadbeater's assertion that through personalisation, consumer 'engagement with a public service should deepen a sense of civic attachment and underpin a sense of citizenship' (Leadbeater, 2004, p 54). It is therefore questionable whether this generalised idea of what a public service is easily applies to adult social care. Many service users argue that current system configurations, eligibility criteria and processes can actively prevent them from exercising their 'citizenship' and do not accord them the consumer power of 'voice and exit' (Rose et al, 2002; Morris, 2004, 2005; Rummery, 2006; Flint, 2009). Nor do they easily provide the conditions for collective (citizen) as well as individual (consumer) action (Scourfield, 2007) – again, a critical dimension for user-led

31

organisations responsible for providing support for direct payment-holders (Davey et al, 2007; Department of Health, 2008; Ipsos MORI, 2011).

Despite personalisation policy claims to 'transform' adult social care, restrictive and exclusionary structures and procedures are being maintained partly because their history and impact has not been properly understood or addressed by policymakers. Such understanding can only come from using or working at the front line of adult social care and mental health services. Beresford is right to question whether the proposed solution of personalisation can work as presently conceived, given the exclusion of those at the front line from participating in the analysis of the problems and their policy solutions. Batmanghelidjh's observation about the problems inherent in the policy proposals for 'Big Society' could therefore also apply to personalisation: 'the difficulty with the … narrative is that unfortunately it's been conceptualised by very bright people who don't always know the dirty spaces of social care' (Batmanghelidjh, 2011).

Up close and personal in Glasgow: the harmful carer, service user and workforce consequences of personalisation

Jim Main

Introduction

The following is a critical reflection on the first year's 'seismic change' (Williams, 2012) implementation of personalisation in Glasgow, which casts doubt on its optimistic claims for service users and workers, and has implications for the Scottish Government's Social Care (Self-directed Support) (Scotland) Bill.[1] The author is a trade union representative with the public sector trade union UNISON in Glasgow.

Personalisation implementation in Glasgow

In 2010, UNISON trade union representatives within Glasgow City Council social work services (SWS) became aware that management were about to introduce self-directed support (SDS), or personalisation as it is more commonly known (HM Government, 2007). The representatives' initial response was to invite a speaker from the Social Worker Action Network (SWAN) to a stewards committee meeting. As well as providing useful information, this helped shape the representatives' critical attitude to personalisation, locating it within the wider austerity cuts agenda, where it was viewed as one aspect of continuing neoliberalism, which seeks to reduce the role of the state, aligned to the Labour Council's own 'modernisation' agenda.[2] Personal budgets shift the risk, cost and responsibility for providing care services from public bodies to individuals (Ferguson, 2007; Whitfield,

2012, pp 18–21). Yet, rather than oppose personalisation *per se*, the representatives argued that service users should have genuine choice regarding service provision and that SDS should not be used to cut care packages.

In September 2010, after consulting with UNISON, Glasgow City Council approved a report to implement personalisation, initially within learning disability services, and then for physically disabled adults. Eventually, SDS will be 'rolled out' to all users of social work services who have a physical or mental health disability (approximately 4,000 in total).

Trade union concerns about the personalisation cuts agenda were confirmed when the council announced that SDS would result in £10 million of savings (11%) from the £89 million social care budget during 2012/13. A senior UNISON branch officer, speaking at a Glasgow Personalisation Network (GPN) meeting, noted: "a quarter of Glasgow's savings, alongside bins, everything has come through personalisation, cuts to disabled services" (GPN meeting, 12 June 2012).

In a press statement, the council regretted that they had been forced to implement spending cuts but stated that SDS would be a fairer system at this 'challenging' time, allowing demand for services to be met 'more quickly and effectively than before':

> it is our view that personalisation of social care offers the best chance for all service users to receive a fair share of the available resources. Personalisation allows for support services to be delivered far more efficiently and this frees up resources that can be directed towards service users looking for support for the first time or those whose support needs have increased. (*Glasgow Local News*, 2012)

The council claimed that personalisation gave service users 'greater say over the support they receive and who provides that support. People clearly indicate to us they welcome the opportunity to take more control over their lives' (*Glasgow Local News*, 2012).

There are 'seven steps' within Glasgow City Council's SDS processes. Initially, social workers and care managers issue a Self Evaluation Questionnaire (SEQ) to service users. Contrary to Simon Duffy's[3] advice that 'one side of A4 is the ideal length for an assessment questionnaire' (Dunning, 2011), the SEQ is a complex multi-page document. It includes questions relating to an individual's: personal care needs; relationships; community integration; ability to make decisions; caring responsibilities; ability to run and maintain their home; ability to stay safe from harm; complex needs and risks; and familial and informal social supports. In each of these areas, respondents are asked to tick boxes that reflect varying support needs, for instance, whether an individual requires 'no support', support 'not every day', support 'several times per week' or 'every day' (Glasgow City Council, 2010). However, a service user could say that they take their own medication when, in reality, it is handed to them. Individuals may say that they are 'fine' when they are just coping (Scottish Parliament, 2012). 'Wrong answers' could reduce SEQ scoring and consequentially the level of services offered.

If service users are unable to complete the SEQ, family members, support workers or advocacy workers can assist completion.[4] When the social worker receives the completed forms, they add their own comments to the service user's, and then enter the forms manually on to a computer programme, a process estimated by some workers to take between four and 10 hours.[5] This activity generates an SEQ score of up to a maximum of 100. From these figures, a £2,000–£70,000 Estimated Budget (EB) is allocated to each service user annually (calculated by the Finance Section). Thereafter, the social worker checks the service user's benefits to ensure that they have been maximised as this figure then determines 'client contribution', resulting in many individuals paying directly for supports for the first time.[6]

The social worker then brings their SEQ and EB to a Resource Allocation Screening Group (RASG), which has a checking and vetting function. This meeting is chaired by a Service Manager, who can apply discretion if, for instance, the carer experiences exceptional stress. In some cases, a Risk Enablement Panel (REP), also chaired by a Service

Manager, takes place to consider the risk implications of resource allocation decisions. Service users and their representatives can attend REPs. In essence, these meetings attempt to balance cost reduction, budgetary pressures and service user vulnerabilities. Inevitably, these aims often come into conflict and there are practitioner concerns that financial prudence is privileged.

When these processes are completed, service users are allocated an actual individual budget to purchase services. In many cases, the budget will continue to fund existing services, but service users whose budget has been reduced will have to decide whether to accept reduced support from an existing provider or move to a cheaper one. Social workers are expected to assist service users to make choices about service providers, but it is unclear at this stage to what extent they become involved in this process. While social workers may be willing to give advice, actively becoming involved and pulling together care provision from a myriad of providers is a complex, contradictory process that can lead to frustrations: the cheapest provider may not be the best.

From the council's perspective, SDS is presented as a rational way to fairly allocate scarce resources in difficult economic times, but there have been concerns that this is a pseudo-scientific process in which, according to a carer, "everything seems random and arbitrary" (GPN meeting, 12 June 2012). A voluntary sector advocacy worker believed that: "In Glasgow, it is like a black box, you ask for some money … and a figure comes out with no explanation" (GPN meeting, 12 June 2012).

Emerging concerns about SDS's negative impact upon service users and the social work and voluntary sector workforces led to the formation of the Glasgow Personalisation Network in July 2011. This brought together service users, carers and a variety of organisations, including the Coalition of Carers, Defend Glasgow Services, the Learning Disability Alliance, SWAN and UNISON Scotland, which organises both council and voluntary sector workers.

In the first six months of 2012, GPN: held a 'hustings' meeting for the May council elections, where candidates where asked for their views on SDS; supported a Green Party councillor's efforts to raise a motion in a full Glasgow City Council meeting, which led to a commitment to 'review' SDS implementation;[7] made a submission to the Scottish Parliament Health and Sport Committee; and organised a major conference on 10 March 2012, which was attended by 90 delegates and several lobbies of the council chambers. SNP councillors are concerned that Glasgow's implementation of SDS could undermine support for the party's Social Care (Self-directed Support) (Scotland) Bill, which will lead to personalisation becoming the norm for service provision throughout Scotland.

Despite personalisation's stated aim to recast users of services as 'citizens' who become 'actively involved in selecting and shaping the services they receive' (Scottish Government, 2009, p 15), the GPN conference heard testimony from many individuals whose lives had been negatively affected by cuts in their care budgets. Service users stated:

> "I've lost 45% of my service. I left home three years ago but now have to spend more time relying on my family ... this makes me feel like a child." (Glasgow service user, 10 March 2012)

> "I'm getting depressed, anxious and lonely and having bad dreams but they won't listen. I feel trapped!" (Glasgow service user, 10 March 2012)

At the conference, carers from the 'Save the Accord' campaign expressed concerns that the closure of the Accord Day Centre in the Dalmarnock area of Glasgow would lead to individuals with learning difficulties no longer receiving a day centre placement. Within the city, some voluntary sector providers have started providing alternative day centre provision for service users who have been told that following a needs reassessment, they can no longer attend the council-run centre, which they may have attended for several years. Campaigners are suspicious that personalisation will exclude individuals with 'lower' or 'less-complex' care needs from services. A worker in a voluntary sector organisation that provides mental health support services expressed commonly held fears: "What we have noticed is the worry that people have, particularly those who need low-level care ... we can't give people answers" (GPN meeting, 12 June 2012).

A service user involved with the Learning Disability Alliance summed up his views of SDS implementation in Glasgow:

"There may be an economic crisis but people with learning difficulties did not cause it. Why should we be asked to pay for it? The Learning Disability Alliance is in favour of more personalised services and so are People First and lots of other organisations. People should have the choice about who supports them. People should have more say over their own lives. People should be left in control. But personalisation in Glasgow has led to people having less choice, less money and less say.... It's not too late for Glasgow Council to sort this problem before it gets any worse." (Service user, Glasgow City Council lobby, 28 June 2012)

Trade union responses

In April 2012, the UNISON union branch organised members' meetings to discuss the workload implications of SDS implementation and thereafter raised several concerns with SWS management relating to the assessment and budget allocation processes, workload management, worker management, and prioritisation. UNISON reported that their social work members viewed SDS implementation timescales 'as totally unrealistic and undermining of good social work practice' (Glasgow City UNISON, 2012). UNISON members gave examples of how scorings were altered by managers against assessors' recommendations, leading to worker conclusions that 'this is primarily a finance/resources led process' (Glasgow City UNISON, 2012). UNISON advised management that 'Members are unhappy at having to inform users and carers of cuts in the allocated budgets. This is undermining morale in SWS' (Glasgow City UNISON, 2012).

—

UNISON union members expressed widespread concerns that they were being asked directly to implement the cuts and, in doing so, are 'somehow expected to justify or explain the £10m personalisation cut for 2012/13 to users and carers' (Glasgow City UNISON, 2012). At management briefings, the council's difficult financial position is emphasised, and SDS is portrayed as a means of mitigating the worst aspect of austerity spending cuts, enabling rational decisions about need to be made that ensure services are fairly spread around. The mantra that 'while some service users with high care packages are reduced, others are increased' is constantly repeated, perhaps to give consolation to sceptical workers.

SDS has led to social work employees experiencing greater work intensification (and work extensification). UNISON reported union member concerns: that some managers were 'over-managing tasks'; that workers were subject to the 'constant monitoring of targets and attendance at RAS[G] meetings'; and about 'inappropriate comments about what will happen if targets are not met, including in some instances threats of disciplinary action'. Social workers have reported that they have felt 'grilled' at RASG meetings and pressured not to advocate on behalf of their clients. In some areas, all work has been allocated irrespective of staffing levels; for management, 'everything is a priority' (Glasgow City UNISON, 2012).

SDS has placed tremendous pressure on workers, with some reporting that they were 'under pressure to do unpaid overtime or paid overtime' (Glasgow City UNISON, 2012). As well as having to cope with a surge in workload arising out of the need to assess new and existing cases to fit the SDS resource allocation criteria, workers had to familiarise themselves with a new computer program, CareFirst 6, while simultaneously working on the older CareFirst 5. In the absence of a workload management scheme, workers reported high stress levels, with one worker stating that 'experienced qualified social workers, who have been around for years, are experiencing worst stress levels ever' (Glasgow City UNISON, 2012).

While some workers accept the common-sense view that 'there is less money in the world', and others accept that they 'have to get on with it' in the hope that it will lead to better outcomes for their clients, others are questioning 'why I am doing the job like this?' (Glasgow City UNISON, 2012). Personalisation firmly shifts social workers' role towards one of 'risk managers and resource allocators, gatekeepers and controllers' (Scottish Government, 2009, p 13), removing any aspects of advocacy and genuine empowerment.

SDS places strain on social workers' relationships with their clients. While the 'council' or 'politicians' could previously be blamed for closing a school or nursery, social workers are now, in effect, the agents directly implementing austerity cuts. Not only do they inform service users of how services are being cut, but *their* assessment has also led to the cut in service. Stewards have reported demoralisation among those workers who first implemented SDS, and there are dangers that this may become pervasive throughout the social care workforce, compounded by job insecurity, a pay freeze and pension concerns.

Faced with conflicting emotional work demands, workers may experience burnout while others resist employer demands by 'working at a cynical distance' (Fleming and Spicer, 2003).To protect themselves, workers detach themselves emotionally from labour processes, while performing work tasks by 'going through the motions'. While this may lead to reduced organisational commitment, worryingly, in an occupation that depends on workers going the 'extra mile', healthy, positive, trusting relationships with service users may be weakened: *I am very sorry you feel the way you do, but there is nothing I can do about it.*

The SEQ assessment facilitates social work's 'distancing' from service users. Previously, community care assessment forms included sections on an individual's personal, family, educational and employment history. This allowed a skilled assessor to provide an assessment that located the service user's physical and mental health needs within a wider context, providing understanding of *who they are*, and *how* and *why* their care needs have changed over time. Community care assessments encouraged a wider holistic assessment rather than the functional 'tick-box' SEQ assessment. Despite Leadbeater's (2004) notion of 'co-production', personalisation's market logic dictates that individuals should no longer be viewed as members of a community

—

with entitlements to services, but as atomised consumers who purchase specific, time-measured, task-oriented services (eg 30 minutes' shopping, one hour's bathing) increasingly provided by the private sector. Social work's retreat from the community in Glasgow is reflected in a shift away from local offices to larger inaccessible 'district'-type offices. This process will be continued further with the introduction of a Social Care Direct call centre.

The UNISON union branch response to this managerial offensive has been to campaign for an independent review of SDS implementation and to demand that the city's £10 million social care budget cut be restored. The union branch has initiated a 'Say No to Overwork' campaign, which attempts to raise awareness of the harmful effects of work-related stress. Shop stewards have advocated the utilisation of a workload management tool that attempts to quantify on a monthly basis what is a reasonable workload given available work hours.

Personalisation has massive implications for the voluntary and private sector social care workforce (Cunningham and Nickson, 2011; Social Value Lab, 2012, p 15). Personalisation's advocates envisage a social care workforce that: is inspired by its goal; is able to 'make a difference' unhindered by red tape and bureaucracy; is 'recognised as collaborators in creating and delivering better care and support'; has high job satisfaction; and is properly rewarded (Self Directed Support Ideas Factory, 2009). However, there are emerging trade union concerns about the emergence of a 'two-tier' workforce, as some employers offer 'zero-hour' contracts (UNISON Scotland, 2012). Generally, social care workers outside of local authorities: have less job security; lack regular hours; are poorly paid; have worse terms and conditions; have less training; have poorer health and safety standards; and are in danger of being pushed towards the 'black economy', with a variety of part-time jobs to meet basic needs (Self Directed Support Ideas Factory, 2009).

In 2011, the wages of workers within Includem, a voluntary sector support provider, were reduced by 9.5%, and UNISON union members within Quarriers took strike action to oppose a 23% pay cut (UNISON Scotland, 2011a). In response to wage-cutting pressures (exacerbated by the introduction of unqualified, unregistered Personal

Assistants), UNISON has urged local councils' commissioning services to write into contracts an obligation that voluntary and private sector providers pay at least the Scottish Living Wage (currently £7.20 per hour).

Discussion

> I believe that in these austere times it is commendable that [through personalisation] this Council has established a process that allocates available resources according to the principles of fairness, equity and transparency. (Councillor Matt Kerr, correspondence, 25 May 2012)

Council managers believe that SDS will stimulate the social care market and result in better outcomes for service users. Managers argue that previous 'block-grant' funding arrangements were inefficient and 'mollycoddled' service users as no longer necessary supports continued to be provided. Irrespective of such claims, attempts to reassess thousands of social care service users in a relatively short period of time have placed considerable pressure on workers, at a time when demand for services is rising. For management, this is a 'challenge'; for service users, it is a time of uncertainty and worry: 'for some personalisation has and will be a positive step forward, for many it represents cuts and a backward step to less choice, less support and less life' (Simon Macfarlane, UNISON Scotland Regional Organiser, correspondence, 18 May 2012).

SDS has also resulted in social workers facing excessive workload demands, with attendant stress (and, in some cases, bullying) pressures as micro-management is extended (Glasgow City UNISON, 2012). Furthermore, workers in the voluntary sector have faced a 'race to the bottom' as their terms and conditions have come under pressure from employers attempting to compete in the new social care market (Social Value Lab, 2012, p 18).

The UNISON union branch approach has been twofold. It vowed to 'step-up its efforts to defend our members from overwork and unacceptable management practices' (Glasgow City UNISON, 2012), while finding common cause with services users and carers affected by personalisation, playing a leading role within the GPN. The GPN conference agreed a statement that placed a series of demands upon Glasgow City Council, which suggests that a different personalisation is possible, one that genuinely 'puts users at the heart of services' and that is delivered by well-paid, well-trained, motivated public and voluntary sector workers. The conference believed that the council should:

- redesign its assessment process to ensure that those with complex needs have those needs fully recognised;
- create real opportunities for individuals and families to reach a consensus with the local authority over the size of their support budgets;
- enable all individuals and their families or their advocates to be part of all allocation meetings that set a budget;
- ensure that there is more flexibility about how social care budgets can be spent – individuals need to be given more scope and responsibility over how they spend their budgets to meet their needs in creative and imaginative ways;
- support more people to have real control over their budgets through setting up or extending support services to help people manage their budgets;
- ensure that all support staff employed through individual budgets are paid the 'Living Wage', whether they are employed by the statutory, voluntary or private sectors or by individuals;
- ensure that the new individual employers understand their role and receive adequate training and support to do this;
- ensure that the employment rights of workers employed through the use of individual budgets are adhered to and that their terms and conditions are broadly similar to those providing care and support in the public sector;
- ensure that all members of the workforce have access to sufficient support and training to carry out their jobs effectively;

- ensure that every personal budget meets all associated employer costs, such as holidays, sickness absence cover and training;
- ensure that carers and family members are recognised as equal partners in care and that they are fully involved in every stage of the process; and
- ensure that carers' own support needs are recognised alongside the needs of the people they care for.

Perhaps, as SDS is extended throughout Scotland, these demands have wider importance and can form the basis for a Personalisation Manifesto. Equally, the common campaigning between service users, carers, disability rights activists and trade unions that produced them can become a model elsewhere. So far, the GPN campaign has not resulted in major changes to how SDS has been implemented, but it has led to greater scrutiny of procedures. Importantly, the campaign has given voice to service users and carers:

> "I used to receive a hundred and sixty hours [of support] a month, I now receive sixty. I don't know what the justification for that is, but there you go ... but I am still here and I am still fighting." (Service user, Glasgow City Council lobby, 28 June 2012)

Postscript (28 August 2012)

Since this response was written in August 2012, the Social Care (Self-directed Support) (Scotland) Bill passed into legislation. Moreover, there is an ongoing campaign to oppose the closure of three learning disability day centres linked to the wider personalisation agenda (see: http://news.stv.tv/west-central/218615-public-react-to-council-decision-to-close-three-glasgow-day-centres/). (For those interested in reading further on this topic, see UNISON Scotland, 2011b.)

Notes

[1] Glasgow City Council introduced self-directed support in advance of the Scottish Government's legislation.

[2] In recent years, the council has pursued a 'Third Way' approach to the provision of services, extending marketisation and commercialisation through housing stock transfer, the introduction of council-controlled arm's-length external organisations – such as Glasgow Life (museums, sport and leisure) and CORDIA (home care and catering) – and the Private Finance Initiative in schools, while still maintaining a reduced core workforce on changed 'single status' employment conditions.

[3] Simon Duffy, when director of In Control between 2003 and 2009, developed the concept of individual or personal budgets.

[4] The limited availability of advocacy services has, in some instances, led to social workers completing the SEQ form for service users.

[5] Some workers have estimated that the SDS process takes between 30 and 40 hours to complete for each individual service user.

[6] Being asked to pay for services may result in some individuals refusing support.

[7] The motion called for SDS implementation to be halted. Cross-party concerns led to an alternative motion being supported, which led to the 'review', although not the fully independent one that GPN called for.

Personalisation – plus ça change?

Alan Roulstone

Beresford provides a warning against any blithe acceptance of new terms in social care and support. He warns against the term 'personalisation' being seen as a new, inherently progressive and irreversible development and language. These assertions are helpful and sobering. So often, newly minted terms in adult social care arise and are aggrandised by use and exchange to take on proportions and promise that cannot be delivered, or that even distort reality. 'Empowerment', 'citizen control', 'user-led services', 'emancipatory practice', all in their time offered new visions or even relations of social support while strangely emanating from a traditional practice and policy context. What makes personalisation different is the apparent borrowing of the language of the Disabled People's Movement and perceived convergence of Department of Health (DH)-driven policy and the more collectively based ideas that sprang from a radical rejection of a paternalist heritage. This convergence could be the result of a genuine listening and response of the DH and an attempt to deliver on the process of capturing the voices of the Disabled People's Movement. Alternatively, personalisation and self-direction can more generally be seen as a cynical use of the term, as a sort of Trojan horse, for obscuring cuts and externalising risk to sick and disabled people in the longer term. For example, by simply changing the language slightly from 'personalisation' to 'personalised solutions', we can undertake a policy sleight of hand that increasingly expects self-determination and self-provisioning to prevail in an era of chronic austerity. This has already happened to some extent in the linguistic shift from 'self-direction' to 'self-management' and in the shift to personalised 'condition management' in the wider policy domain.

The truth is somewhere between these points, I would argue. I fully agree with Beresford's concern that personalisation does not enter the lexicon of policy and practice without health warnings. There have undoubtedly been genuine attempts to listen to organisations of disabled people and personalisation is clearly a counter to paternalist Fordist principles that services will be delivered according to professional needs and not those of service users. However, the term and its use risk becoming post-Fordist in the sense that limited funding and the spending of meagre budgets on essentials, rather than transforming social care, may simply be the equivalent of changing the outer appearance of disabled people's lives. In this sense, personalisation in its purest sense has to be seen as synonymous with greater personal determination and choice-making. Behind such a 'pure model' of personalisation are the following substantiating conditions of personalisation, without which the term is, at best, a distraction and, at worst, a form of one-dimensional obfuscation of the truth:

1. That the social relations of support are shifted in a way that ensures that choice and control are not the end result of a disempowered and depersonalised assessment and eligibility process.
2. That the term only approaches imagined policy ideals if the wider social support system is humane, equitable and personalised.
3. That ideological and linguistic distortion do not shift personalisation to a position of being the handmaiden of de-collectivised life. The latter arguably being a key facet of neoliberalism.

The origins and ideological precursors of personalisation will continue to be hotly debated. It is important, however, not to dismiss personalisation outright, as another term will likely take its place – one run through with the same levels of ambiguity and ideological fudge that bedevils much disability policy. Similarly, any prophetic and uncritical use risks simply shifting many disabled people from an enforced collectivism to an enforced individualism. As academics, however, we do need to continue to research personalisation in practice and as a lived experience in order to document the unravelling of

---

the term. It is the nature of power and ideology that the true nexus of power is not revealed until ideas, words and policy directions are fundamentally challenged. Perhaps only when enough evidence emerges that personalisation is being experienced very differently and the term is in jeopardy will powerful forces emerge to reconstruct the contested terrain of social care and support. Having said that, the term does have its uses, for example, where it is being used to accurately reflect on genuine new choice-making and a redrawing of the professional–service user power relationship.

Although funding for adult social care research has arguably never been so conservative in nature and the funding pattern of the NIHR (National Institute for Health Research) School for Social Care so narrow, there is scope for researchers to explore personalisation in their local contexts against the backdrop of severe cuts in adult social care. It is axiomatic that to talk uncritically of personalised and responsive social care at a time that most sick and disabled people cannot get access to support is a cruel irony. In this sense, as point 2 in the earlier list suggests, it would be one-dimensional language and policy analysis to talk of personalised adult social care when the 'Fair' Access to Care guidance (itself an increasingly Orwellian term) has been inverted to only offer eligibility to the highest category of need in the majority of local contexts. How can social support be personalised if the wider system operates in a very depersonalised way, denying many people access to any adult social care support? Academics and practitioners have to be aware of this particular 'language game'.

It is tempting to reject the term 'personalisation' outright. Its associations with a neoliberal era is a warning; however, it is not sufficient grounds to reject the term as it emanated from a complex set of dynamics that would not unravel by a simple change of nomenclature. Arguably, what are being debated are continued problems with the epiphenomena of the social care and support system. A change of language will not alter that. However, a contestation of the term is crucially important, as is a similar challenging of practice tenets around personalised support. This is made especially piquant by the decline of the global economy. Some services will manage, largely

—

via street-level creativity, to ensure small *islands of personalisation*. What we do not have is a system of *personalised social support* and we need to guard against any linguistic and policy slippage towards a misuse of the latter term.

The need for true person-centred support

Pat Stack

With a season ticket for Rochdale FC, some air conditioning and grace-and-favour curries, the personalisation agenda was hailed as 'the new way forward for social care'. Such was the excitement of its champions, the enthusiasm of the Department of Health and even the acquiescence of one or two disability organisations close to the ear of the government, that it felt impolite, if not downright obstructive, to raise any questions and concerns about the agenda.

Therefore, when the London Direct Payments Forum (since rebranded the London Self-Directed Support Forum) called a conference raising concerns, we were met with some criticism. In Control, a driving force behind personalisation, chose not to attend, and some other enthusiasts came reluctantly when the sheer breadth of the speakers made it impossible to avoid.

The conference ('If we're going to do it – do it right') involved a wide variety of speakers, including some of the most enthusiastic proponents of personalisation and some of its most sceptical critics. One of the key speakers was Peter Beresford. His insightful and critical articles in *The Guardian* and elsewhere may not have been warmly welcomed by some forums but for a conference such as ours, his involvement was a must.

The point of the conference was neither to rubbish nor laud the proposals, but to guard against doing the thing badly. Those of us who had worked around direct payments for years were keen to avoid the mistakes of the past, where due to the random way in which the schemes were introduced into the different areas, some fine practice in some places contrasted with the most shameful practices in others.

We had seen just how long it had taken the worst to get anywhere near the best.

From the beginning, there were concerns. From the point of view of those of us that had worked around direct payment support, there was real concern that that support appeared to be largely written out of the new process, the implication being that family members would/should provide what is often highly specialised and very time-consuming support. Furthermore, the oft-mentioned innovations cited at the beginning of this piece, while good, were highly specific initiatives, dangerous to generalise from and, as with most pilots, resourced in ways that were often unlikely to be met in general practice.

The freedom to use funds 'without the bureaucratic restrictions of Direct Payments' has largely proved illusory as cash-starved local authorities become more keen to recoup funds, more obsessed with 'misuse' and, in some cases, more intrusive into care arrangements. Furthermore, the much-heralded new processes have run into trouble. The Supported Self Assessment, which was meant to give users a much bigger say, has often proved in practice to be an unwieldy questionnaire with tick boxes that fail to 'individualise' the service user's needs.

On top of that, the 'Resource Allocation System' (RAS) was enthusiastically introduced as a transparent way of allocating care, but, in reality, is often a more opaque system, leaving care practitioners scratching their heads as they try to explain why a substantial care package has been slashed by a computer calculation. Of course, it was not the fault of personalisation champions that the bankers threw the world into economic turmoil, but it was the championing of 'cost-effectiveness' that has seen many local authorities seize on the process as a cost-cutting exercise.

Lastly, as Beresford cites, over £1 billion was handed to local authorities, who almost drowned themselves in a wave of consultants (in very few cases taken from user or disability movement sources), and who having spent the best part of two years training and cajoling staff in new processes, finally either abandoned them or changed them out of all recognition.

In his conclusion, Beresford quite rightly argues that the way forward is the implementation of 'true person-centred support'. We have to build on the success of direct payments and overcome their shortcomings, but for that to happen, as Beresford argues with great insight, initiative and control has to come from below, not be imposed from above.

.

All in the name of personalisation

Helga Pile

Whenever UNISON members working in adult social care gather to talk about personalisation some key themes crop up:

- window-dressing for cuts;
- additional bureaucracy;
- reduced social work involvement;
- loss of local services and jobs; and
- increase in safeguarding concerns.

Day centres being closed, meals on wheels services being cut, management pressure to trim care packages – all these are being done in personalisation's name.

Councils are focusing their efforts on hitting the crude target of everyone on a personal budget, while facing growing need with shrinking resources. The direct consequence is the strangling of the principles of empowerment and control in a tangle of bureaucracy. Resource allocation systems, in all their complexity, make rights more difficult to keep in focus, and rationing easier to disguise.

As Peter Beresford has pointed out, personalisation is a policy that has been sold by anecdote. But it is proving much harder to get an airing for the anecdotes that practitioners are telling us, for example:

- The elderly parents and carers of a learning-disabled man who used to attend a day centre five days a week. Now the centre is closed, he has a direct payment that is only enough to pay for a support worker to take him out a few hours a week. The rest of the week, he is at home, bored and his parents are finding it hard to cope.

- The disabled woman who has a direct payment that pays for a team of personal assistants (PAs). Things are getting very difficult as one of the PAs (a UNISON member) has been injured at work but the woman does not believe that it is her responsibility to have employers' liability insurance, and the council is not helping to resolve the issue.

Practitioners responding to a UNISON survey[1] felt that they were implementing a 'one-size-fits-all' approach to personalisation, driven by sign-up targets. This has been exacerbated by the 2010 announcement by government ministers in England[2] that 'direct payments should be the preferred option' for receiving a personal budget. Respondents do not feel that this is real personalisation because the focus is on process not outcomes.

Practitioners are clear that to deliver genuine personalisation requires additional time and input from social workers – time they have not got as staffing levels are cut while need and levels of demand continue to rise:

> "I believe there are some positives to be gained from the individual budgets, especially for the service user, such as greater autonomy and empowerment. I do not necessarily believe it will deskill social workers but I believe there is a hope that the service will save money and time with these budgets, which would be untrue." (UNISON social worker)

A UNISON/*Community Care* survey in May 2011 found that only 20% of practitioners have enough time with service users to effectively support self-assessment; fewer than half (45%) said that service users are given enough support to manage their personal budgets.

The bureaucratic load being created by personalisation is considerable – and this is disappointing considering the claims that it would herald empowerment and liberation for practitioners. Our 2011 survey found 73% of practitioners saying that personalisation has resulted in more bureaucracy for them in their role:

Administrative demands accompanying the new self-directed support (SDS) process have increased threefold in comparison to the previous system.... The vast majority of individuals feel that the process is so mystifying and daunting that they immediately request that all forms are processed by their social care assessor.... Consequence: severe service capacity issues, lowering of staff morale, disempowerment resulting in lose–lose outcomes for staff and individuals.... Ethical issues also arise since the documentation purports to be written in the first person (regardless of whether the person has capacity issues). (UNISON branch East Midlands: letter to management)

For those needing personal care in their own homes – particularly the elderly – personal budgets are barely enough to cover basic needs. They certainly do not stretch to the leisure and social activities that so many would like access to. If the traditional funding approach (which does at least generate economies of scale) increasingly only buys a couple of 15-minute visits from a minimum-wage home care agency, how can 'transformation' be achieved by giving less cash to an individual and saying sort something better out yourself?

Personalisation has heralded a whole new round of that local government perennial: restructuring. Dovetailing with the austerity cuts, this has led to widespread moves to reduce the number of qualified social workers and occupational therapists employed, and replace them with 'cheaper' staff, such as 'support workers':

"As I have worked as a Social Work Assistant initially for 12 years and as a Community Care Worker/Care Manager since 1992, I have obviously built up a great deal of expertise.... I have had many line managers over the years and although they initially start by attempting to screen the complexity of cases that are allocated to me, the situation generally evolves into being asked to take cases of equal complexity as the Registered Social Workers." (UNISON social work assistant[3])

Practitioners have consistently expressed the view that the emphasis on the numbers set up with personal budgets, and the shortage of capacity and excessive caseloads in the service, are increasing levels of risk to service users. A Serious Case Review report by Buckinghamshire Safeguarding Vulnerable Adults Board[4] concluded:

> Regrettably, social worker expertise was not deployed – not even in a professional advisory capacity....
>
> It appears that the way that social workers undertook their role meant that it promoted access to Direct Payments without professional challenge as to need, appropriateness or outcome....
>
> Perhaps this inattention reflects naivety regarding potential problems in the delivery of Direct Payments; and/or the absence of healthy professional scepticism about human behaviour and motivations; and/or inexperience; and/or targets to keep the numbers of Direct Payments recipients climbing forever upwards. Direct Payments are a process and not an outcome.

Looking to the future, personalisation has lost much of its promise. Many practitioners feel that the ideal of personalisation is a lost dream. That leaves them – working through their UNISON branches – with the challenge of finding effective ways to combat what is going on in personalisation's name, and to promote progressive alternatives.[5] Furthermore, there are a number of policy developments that look set to create further complexity and scope for fragmentation: the prospect of GP commissioning consortia and their interrelationship with social care; the pilot of personal budgets into health premised on the 'success anecdotes' from social care; and a broadening spectrum of privatisation from multinationals to mutuals.

Is there an alternative? Personalisation should not be built around the supremacy of the transaction, but the supremacy of the service user's rights. Service users and practitioners need to work together to expose and reject the version of personalisation that is being served up, and develop a new one based on what service users want, and what works:

"[The most satisfying thing about my job is] supporting service users to maintain a satisfactory level of independence (where possible) – advocating on their behalf to ensure that their needs are being met. Working with new people and promoting them to continue living their lives the way they want to. Being person-centred – with the service user's needs, wants, wishes as the main priority." (UNISON support worker)

Notes

[1] UNISON, 'Not waving but drowning: paperwork and pressure in adult social work services', August 2009.

[2] Department of Health, *A vision for adult social care: capable communities and active citizens*, 2010.

[3] UNISON, 'Stepping into the breach – social work's paraprofessionals', September 2011.

[4] Buckinghamshire's Safeguarding Vulnerable Adults Board, 'Executive summary: the Murder of Mr C, A Serious Case Review', May 2011.

[5] See UNISON, 'Up close and personal, a toolkit for branches dealing with personalisation in social care', 2011.

Personalisation – is there an alternative?

Roddy Slorach

By any measure, personalisation has not been a success. There is widespread confusion as to its purpose, a marked unevenness in its implementation and a veritable chasm between government rhetoric on the issue and the harsh reality of its practical application. Crucially, the context in which it is being imposed is making any future success increasingly unlikely – at least for most service providers and (often, would-be) users.

In April 2013, a series of major benefits cuts began, representing 'the biggest contraction in Britain's welfare state since its foundation in the 1940s'.[1] As Sue Marsh has put it:

> imagine what might happen if all of these cuts affect you at once. No carer to help at home, no ESA [Employment and Support Allowance] to replace your lost income, no car to get about and no support to stay in your own home. What might have been manageable becomes the most terrible, frightening scenario possible. Without these vital elements of your life, you are left with nothing; bedridden, housebound, isolated and living in crushing poverty. Add in cuts to housing benefit and the NHS, and it doesn't take much imagination to see that the results could be devastating.[2]

The restrictions to Housing Benefit include the 'bedroom tax'. Its first-known victim, Stephanie Bottrill, left a suicide note that simply said: 'The only people to blame are the government'.[3] The Independent Living Fund, which tops up council social care packages for those most severely disabled, has been closed to new clients, and will be scrapped completely from 2015 onwards. It has been estimated that the cuts to benefits and services will rob 3.7 million disabled people of £28 billion by 2017/18.[4] The human costs are, of course, much harder to calculate.

Even before most of these cuts were announced, the Joint Parliamentary Committee on Human Rights believed there to be 'inadequate legal safeguards to protect and promote the right to independent living'.[5] The Supreme Court, meanwhile, upheld the right of Kensington and Chelsea Council (the UK's richest borough) to leave a disabled woman lying in her bed wearing incontinence pads for 12 hours each night, rather than supplying her with the help that she needs to use the toilet.[6]

Many families providing care are being pushed to breaking point. A report by Age UK says that there are 800,000 people in England with care needs who receive no formal support.[7] Others face losing their homes and savings because of soaring care bills.

Turning rebellion into money

In July 2010, Health Secretary Andrew Lansley, in a keynote speech about the NHS and Social Care Bill, claimed that his 'guiding principle will be "no decision about me, without me"', and that he would 'extend personal budgets, giving patients with long-term conditions real choices about their care'. This tactic – the cynical use of the language of disability rights to undermine their substance – is not new. In 2006, two of the UK disability movement's best-known figures observed that 'a combination of Government and the big charities have successfully adopted the big ideas of the disabled people's movement, usurped its language, and undertaken further initiatives which promise much yet deliver little'.[8] So, the replacement for Disability Living Allowance is likely to make anyone 'successfully' using aids and adaptations ineligible for the new Personal Independence Payment – as such 'independence' renders them ineligible for further state support (Morris, 2011).

Peter Beresford is right to say that personalisation contrasts sharply in both origins and approach from that of direct payments. The latter

—

was campaigned for by a disability movement demanding real choice and control over their lives, instead of being dependent on charity – or on a welfare state that similarly took little or no account of their wishes. But, as Jenny Morris says, these demands:

> resonated with the Conservative Government's agenda; and drew attention to the way a lack of choice and control could undermine human rights, which then fitted well with New Labour's agenda. We have, unintentionally, contributed towards a steady undermining of collective responsibility and redistribution. (Morris, 2011)

By the mid-1990s, the disability movement had passed its mobilising peak, its leaders increasingly focusing on legislative change as the means of achieving its founding aim of independent living.

Targeting resources in social care at those deemed 'most vulnerable' has meant in practice a cumulative narrowing of eligibility criteria and increased means testing to identify those who should be made to pay for their own care. In October 2012, the government's own figures showed that although 43% of eligible people have a budget, only a minority take this as a direct cash payment.[9] The target requiring councils in England to give all users of social services a personal budget was subsequently dropped. Many service users do not want to manage their own budget or become an employer, with all the complexity and stress that this would involve. The priority, especially among the elderly, is for a decent-quality service provided by properly trained and motivated staff.

What is the alternative?

The central problem facing those who wish to resist the onslaught on our public services is the political consensus shared by all three main parties, and even by many leading figures in the trade unions. This posits that there is no alternative to huge cuts in public spending for the foreseeable future, and that welfare spending is therefore both

—

unsustainable and nourishes a culture of 'dependency' among benefit claimants and service users.

There are proposals that can and should be put to try and make personalisation work in practice, and there are (rare) examples where it has been done. But, as the Care and Support Alliance put it, 'personal budgets are easier to cut than existing services and responsibility can be placed on individuals to achieve "efficiency savings"'.[10] In the context of austerity and a general assault on social spending, only fundamental social and economic change can deliver social care worthy of the name. Beresford rightly says that there is no golden age to retreat to, but is there really 'no preferable alternative'? We need to start by asking how we can implement 'true person-centred support' in practice.

In a society driven primarily by profit, recessions mean pressures to further exclude and penalise those who can no longer, or can only in limited ways, generate that profit. Policies of wealth redistribution may be unfashionable for some, but only a break from free market orthodoxies – themselves a throwback to Victorian times – can provide the resources necessary to build a truly inclusive society.

There remains a huge loyalty to the welfare state as well as huge potential for serious resistance to defend it – and an urgent need to act on this. Such resistance would then enable service users and providers to work together to develop new and democratically accountable ways of both developing and delivering services. Modest examples of such alliances already exist in grassroots campaigns against the cuts. More than ever, we need the old collective principle of 'from each according to their ability, and to each according to their needs'.

Notes

[1] *Financial Times*, 1 April 2013. Available at: http://www.ft.com/cms/s/0/f88c2f28-977a-11e2-b7ef-00144feabdc0.html#axzz2PsSrgGRE

[2] Sue Marsh, *The Guardian*, 9 July 2013. Available at: http://www.guardian.co.uk/commentisfree/2013/jul/09/disabled-people-cuts-cumulative-impact

[3] *The Daily Mirror*, 13 May 2013. Available at: http://www.mirror.co.uk/news/uk-news/bedroom-tax-suicide-stephanie-bottrills-1886058

[4] *The Guardian*, 27 March 2013. Available at: http://www.guardian.co.uk/society/2013/mar/27/welfare-cuts-disabled-people?INTCMP=SRCH

[5] Jane Campbell, *The Guardian*, 1 March 2012. Available at: http://www.guardian.co.uk/commentisfree/2012/mar/01/disabled-people-have-come-far?INTCMP=SRCH

[6] See: http://www.supremecourt.gov.uk/docs/UKSC_2011_0005_Judgment.pdf

[7] BBC News, 30 January 2012. Available at: http://www.bbc.co.uk/news/health-16743231

[8] Mike Oliver and Colin Barnes, 'Disability politics and the disability movement in Britain: where did it all go wrong?', first published in *Coalition* (Greater Manchester Coalition of Disabled People, August 2006).

[9] *The Guardian*, 26 October 2012. Available at: http://www.guardian.co.uk/society/2012/oct/26/councils-social-services-personal-budget?INTCMP=SRCH

[10] From: http://careandsupportalliance.files.wordpress.com/2011/12/care-support-alliance-engagement-exercise-submission3.pdf

Personal budgets: the two-legged stool that doesn't stand up

Colin Slasberg

The strategy to deliver personalisation through personal budgets using a process conceived by the charity In Control was ushered in with expectations few would argue against:

- *A new way to allocate resources that would be both fair and transparent.* This would be delivered through a Resource Allocation System (RAS) to replace the capricious 'professional gift' system (Duffy, 1996).
- *Savings through a reduced level of bureaucracy.* With service users carrying out their own support planning, there would be less need for assessment and care management (Leadbeater, 2008).
- *Greater control for service users.* This was the overriding vision, and would end the domination of support planning by the menu of pre-purchased services.

These expectations form three tests that, between them, can be used to evaluate the degree of success of the strategy. Five years of implementation has provided a fund of evidence to do so.

Has it changed the way resources are allocated?

The up-front allocation is meant to be 'indicative' of how much the person is entitled to. This is to allow any minor adjustment that might be needed to ensure eligible needs can be met. As such, the indicative and actual allocations should be 'as close as possible' (TLAP, 2011) to each other. Measuring the difference between the indicative and actual

—

allocations therefore offers a test of whether the RAS is in reality a new way to allocate resources.

There is no routine collection of either of these sets of data. However, Freedom of Information requests can produce the data. The largest of these was carried out by the London Self-Directed Support Forum (2013). All 33 London councils were asked for the indicative and actual allocations for all new service users for the year 2011/12, resulting in the following findings:

- 21 of the 33 councils could not provide the data as they did not collect it. This was surprising as there is clear advice from the Association of Directors of Adult Social Services (2010) to collate the data in order to continuously monitor and adjust the RAS. It suggests that these authorities may not be regarding the up-front allocation as seriously as expected.
- For those that did provide data, the difference was measured as a ratio, whereby if they were the same, the ratio was 1. It was found that the average ratio was 2.6. This means that with an indicative budget of £100, if the actual was more, it would on average be £260; if it was less, it would on average be £40.

Differences of this order point to the actual allocation being made *independently* of the up-front allocation, not guided by it. This finding was corroborated by Series and Clements (2013). They carried out a detailed analysis of how the RAS worked in 20 councils. They concluded that the RAS was a 'poor indicator' of how much people actually required, and that it was like 'a cog spinning in a machine with which it does not connect' (Series and Clements, 2013, p 20).

Series and Clements argue that compliance with the law would, indeed, rule out allowing the RAS to determine how much a person receives. They refer to Supreme Court judgments (*KM v Cambridgeshire*) which make clear that a council must know the particular needs of the person and the most reasonable costs of meeting them before making a decision. To this imperative can be added a council's imperative to spend within its budget. Councils are not likely to offer people more

—

than is required to meet the needs they have agreed to fund. Evidence of this dynamic being at play is that in the survey of London councils, for every occasion the actual budget was more than the indicative budget, there were two occasions when it was less. Thus, the evidence is clear that the RAS has not changed the way resources are allocated, and so the strategy fails the first test.

Has bureaucracy reduced?

There is anecdotal evidence that far from reducing bureaucracy, it has increased it. *Community Care* magazine carries out an annual survey of its readers' experience of the strategy. In 2013, 78% agreed that bureaucracy had increased.

Hard data in the form of national data returns (see: National Adult Social Care Intelligence System at: https://nascis.ic.nhs.uk) also exists to test this question by measuring changes in productivity. If bureaucracy is reducing, it can be expected that productivity would increase. The key comparison is between the years 2007/08 and 2011/12. This shows the following:

- there has been an increase in staffing in fieldwork by 8.4%;[1]
- there has been a reduction in the major activities of assessment and care management (assessments, reviews and separate carer assessments) of 16.5%; and
- there has been a reduction of people receiving 'professional support' (social work support beyond care management) of 47%.

If it is assumed that each of the four main fieldwork activities mentioned require equal amounts of time, the preceding would show a loss of productivity of 26.9%. This loss coincides with the implementation of the personal budget strategy and resonates both with the anecdotal evidence and with the evidence that the RAS has not replaced the prevailing system of resource allocation, but merely been an addition to it. Therefore, it is reasonable to believe that the strategy does not just fail the second test, but has actually increased bureaucracy very significantly.

Has the strategy increased service user control?

A new reporting requirement for councils in 2011/12 was the extent to which people feel in control of their lives. Although the overall national targets for the percentage of service users said to have a personal budget have been met, there is significant variation between individual councils. This creates an opportunity to test the extent to which the strategy is leading to service users experiencing greater control. A scattergram can be used to plot two variables against one another to establish the relationship between them through what is called the trendline. This device can be used to plot the percentage of people who said they have control over their lives against the percentage of people said to have a personal budget for each council. Proponents of the personal budget strategy would hope to see that as the percentage of people with a personal budget increases, so would the percentage who say they have control over their lives. However, that is not the case. There is, indeed, a slight trend in the opposite direction. This evidence points to the strategy failing the third test, and therefore all three.

Government perception

The government continues to believe that the strategy is the right one to pursue, and continues to set targets for the numbers of people with a personal budget arrived at through an up-front allocation. However, it also acknowledges that it has not been universally welcomed, and believes that the problem is that not all councils have delivered the strategy correctly.

The evidence that drives this view is provided by Think Local Act Personal, a body funded by the government to promote the strategy, and In Control. These are, therefore, not independent sources. Of particular relevance is a national survey – the Personal Budgets

Outcome Evaluation Tool (POET) – of people said to be personal budget-holders. It has reported twice, the second time in May 2013 (Hatton and Waters, 2013). Twenty volunteer councils identified some 2,000 respondents, with most reporting that they experienced better outcomes. Also, where better outcomes were not achieved, this was related to poorer experience of the process. However, the following facts are key to a proper interpretation:

- Of the respondents, 89% had some form of direct payment. This contrasts with just 10% nationally. There has been evidence of better outcomes being achieved by direct payment users since they were introduced in the mid-1990s.
- The 11% of respondents without a direct payment – 'council-managed' budget-holders – are the real test of the personal budget strategy as they experience only the new innovation of the up-front allocation. POET points out that these respondents also said that their personal budget improved their outcomes. However, the following factors must be taken into account:
  - The question asked fails to isolate the process used to secure services from the actual services. This means that respondents were not comparing having a personal budget with any other process of getting a service, but compared actually having *the services* purchased with having no services. This may be the case for all respondents, but is inescapably true for the several respondents that had not even experienced any other process with which they could compare.
  - The report tested for statistical significance of the relationship between the 14 outcome measures used and (among other factors) whether people had a direct payment or council-managed budget. The tables showed that council-managed budgets did not have a statistically significant positive relationship with a single outcome measure across the four user groups, but they did have statistically significant negative relationships with 14.

- While the report notes that councils varied by up to 30% in the extent to which people reported better outcomes, it was also the case that there was a similar variation (up to 40%) in the percentage of each council's sample with a direct payment.

The government has also used the evaluation of the Personal Health Budgets (Forder et al, 2012) pilots as evidence that a strategy based on up-front allocation is right. Over a three-year period, at 20 sites who were given £100,000 each year, the outcomes of some 1,000 people said to have been a given personal health budget were compared with a similar number who were not. In the majority of cases, those with a personal health budget enjoyed better outcomes. Thus, Julie Stansfield, Chief Executive of In Control, in an article for *The Guardian* (Stansfield, 2013), said:

> Crucially, the findings about what works replicated those in social care. To achieve the best results, personal budgets must be delivered according to the principles of self-directed support – that is, people need to know the budget they have to plan their care with, be able to choose the mechanism for managing the budget and have maximum flexibility in use of budgets.

However, this is a misrepresentation of the facts. The evaluation report identified sites using four models of delivery. One of the models did not apply an up-front allocation, yet the sites that used this model still achieved the better outcomes. The other three groups did claim to offer an up-front allocation. Of those, one did not achieve the better outcomes. This led the evaluation team to the following conclusion: 'possibly ... it is the greater choice and flexibility that is more important than knowing the budget level' (Forder et al, 2012, p 76).

Conclusions

The In Control process to deliver personal budgets through up-front allocations rested largely on un-evidenced assertions. However, it resonated powerfully with prevailing political belief systems that emphasised the pursuit of individual preference by financially empowered consumers as the route to better public services, with the promise of cost savings. It was eagerly adopted as policy, even before the government's own evaluation reported. When it did report, there were clear warning signs. Not only was the evidence of better outcomes far from unequivocal, but there were early warnings of major increases in infrastructure costs. It is perhaps no surprise, therefore, that evidence is now building rapidly to show that the strategy is failing against any of the tests that it can reasonably be expected to be measured against, and that the thinking was fundamentally flawed. Continuing belief that the strategy is working perhaps owes much to those who backed the strategy being willing to hear only evidence that it is.

Note

[1] Relevant data exist for staff numbers that enable comparison between 2007/08 and 2011/12. These showed an increase of 8.6%. However, the return changed for 2012/13, making comparison no longer possible. However, it is known that spending on fieldwork reduced by 1.7%. If it is assumed that this was due to an equivalent reduction in staffing, the increase in staffing since 2007/08 would be reduced to 8.4%.

Once more on personalisation

Peter Beresford

As the original inflated claims of the proponents of personal budgets and personalisation are subjected to critical examination, so we can see the policy's foundations and knowledge base crumbling around us. As time passes, the picture gets worse, not better. It is difficult not to be struck by the solipsism of this development, which was embarked upon casually and without independent evidence. This in a policy area – social care – that has long been beset with problems and where the consequences for the many thousands of service users dependent upon it could be and often have been damaging and even life-threatening.

However, the responsibility for this ill-conceived and poorly evidenced policy really has to be lain at the door of the politicians and policymakers who rushed to implement it. There are always enthusiasts who will over-claim for their pet projects. It is the job of policymakers to negotiate such difficulties. In this case, the promise of getting better for less, in a chronically underfunded field of policy, clearly overrode ministers' better judgement.

As one of this book's contributors, Helga Pile, reminds us, discussion about personalisation has never been an inclusive or equal one. Some voices, notably, the voices pushing determinedly for it, have consistently been privileged. As she observes, the policy was sold on anecdote, but practitioners were not given an equal hearing. Nor, indeed, were service users, or carers, analysts or activists who did not take the party line.

This book represents an exception to that rule. Here, instead, diverse and critical voices, voices of experience, have been given the chance to offer their views on the theory and practice of personal budgets and personalisation. Here, a much richer and more critical and helpful picture emerges.

First, we are given warts-and-all accounts of some of the realities behind the implementation of the policy. Thus, Jim Main sets out the way in which the move to personalisation in Glasgow has been strongly associated with reductions in support and increases in bureaucratisation, while wrongly rationalised by its leaders as a way of fairly distributing (reduced) resources. Accounts from Pat Stack, Sarah Carr and Helga Pile highlight the top-down nature of the reform, which has frequently excluded practitioners, service users and carers. Hailed as making possible a customised service, it has instead increasingly been tied to targets and bureaucratic measures of 'performance'. It has been used to justify and smokescreen cuts in services and jobs at a time of radical social policy change that has meant service users are even more in need of the advocacy role of social work.

Colin Slasberg offers a carefully evidenced discussion that shows convincingly that the two legs upon which conventional and prevailing approaches to personal budgets and 'self-directed support' have rested – 'upfront allocation' and the Resource Allocation System' – fail on all claimed counts.

Accounts here also highlight complexity. Thus, Alan Roulstone warns against throwing out the baby with the bathwater. He helpfully highlights and analyses issues of linguistics, ideology and power in relation to how personalisation and personal budgets have been constructed by different interests. He and others call for more and better research – since if we are not working for real 'personalisation' or person-centred support, what other goal is there? It is not the goals or explicit aspirations of personalisation and personal budgets that writers here are critical of, but the systems that have actually been implemented supposedly to achieve them. Sarah Carr dissects the damaging role in this reform of the ideologue Charles Leadbeater, one of the most influential voices. His top-down approach, based on his earlier ideas of the 'citizen-consumer' and 'social entrepreneurship', ungrounded and untested in this context, have excluded service users, devalued practitioners and held a central role for top-down planners like himself.

Despite all the emerging problems, however, the current national narrative still seems to be that the personal budget strategy is progressing well. The October 2012 reduction in the target for those with a personal budget from 100% to 70% by April 2013 has been described as no more than a minor adjustment to the pace of change, with the minister calling the new target a 'staging post, not a ceiling'. There is still official talk of personal budgets for all.

However, this positive view is fundamentally challenged by a growing body of evidence (Slasberg et al, 2012a, 2012b, forthcoming[a], forthcoming[b]). This points to a very different reality, and indicates that the positive narrative has been maintained by the use of highly selective and unrepresentative information. This evidence leads to the following conclusions about current policy and practice:

- Improved outcomes are only experienced by people who use a direct payment to self-manage their support system. Personal budgets, defined as they are by an 'up-front' allocation, make no contribution to improved outcomes.
- The finding that personal budgets improve outcomes has been achieved by 'packing' survey samples with people with a direct payment, making them quite unrepresentative. The 2011 National Survey of 2,000 'personal budget-holders' consisted of nearly 90% with a direct payment at a time when, nationally, only 7.7% of service users had one.
- Up-front allocations are not driving resource allocations as intended or claimed. The legal and financial risks mean that they are never likely to. Far from 50% of people having a personal budget as claimed, the truer statement is that they may not exist at all as currently defined.
- Nonetheless, with the numbers that councils say have an up-front allocation being the sole determinant of the extent to which they are held to be delivering the personalisation agenda, councils have

invested hugely in delivering them. Staff levels are up by some 10%, while productivity (numbers of assessments, reviews and people supported by social workers) is down by an even greater level. This means that in addition to the £500 million development money between 2008 and 2011 being spent to create systems that do not work, what could be as much as a further £500 million a year is being lost to service a bureaucracy that has no actual benefit.

- While it is claimed that the better outcomes achieved by people with direct payments are due to a better process, it is more likely that they are due in large measure to them having sufficient resources. At the time of the National Survey, while only 7.7% of people had a direct payment, they used 13.7% of the spend on community support between them. This different rate of spending is not explained by complexity of need. Direct payments are open to all, and there are some with small packages of support. There is no evidence that they have 'too much', but more that they have enough to meet all their relevant needs. This is in stark contrast to the majority who usually do not.

- The recent expansion in the numbers with a direct payment – up from about 5% of all service users before the strategy to about 11% – is not likely to consist of people who will experience the same higher levels of outcome. The growth has not been matched by what should have been a reduction in the provision of mainstream services if they employed their own supports. This points to the new group being people who simply have a bank account and ability to pay bills. However, they have no desire to manage their own support system.

This pattern of using information in a way that promotes a positive view of the national strategy has continued:

- In 2012, Skills for Care reported a massive expansion in the numbers of personal assistants now being employed by direct payment recipients. However, there are no actual returns upon which to base their data. Their figures are based entirely on a sample from some years ago which said that people with a direct payment employ 2.35 personal assistants each. They then made the assumption that every new direct payment recipient would employ their own personal assistants. At the same time, they report that the number of jobs in mainstream domiciliary care – for which there is actual data – has also increased. They have not acknowledged that it cannot be the case that both statements are true (Skills for Care, 2012).

• The Office of Public Management reported a three-year longitudinal study from Essex showing that personal budgets were greatly improving outcomes. However, the study in its third year involved a mere 29 service users, all of whom were direct payment recipients selected three years ago (OPM, 2012).

Contributors to this book approach personalisation and personal budgets in a very different way, grounded in the experience of how it is actually working. They emphasise the importance of a bottom-up approach if personalisation is to work effectively. Most explicitly make this point. Pat Stack says that it must be a process that centrally involves service users. Roddy Slorach asks how we can implement true person-centred support in practice. He sees this as part of a bigger project to build a grassroots defence of the welfare state and public services. He argues for inclusive campaigns and effective alliances with service users and providers, who should be supported to pioneer new accountable ways to develop and deliver services. Jim Main calls for local demands to be identified as the basis for a 'personalisation manifesto'. Helga Pile makes the case for service users and workers to work together to meet the service users' and carers' rights and needs. Alan Roulstone sets out principles and conditions for *positive* personalisation.

There is a remarkable unanimity of view among the contributors within these covers, even though they come from a wide range of perspectives, including service users, practitioners, researchers, academics and trade unionists. They make it possible to redress the balance in discussions about personalisation and personal budgets by helping to open them up. Perhaps most important, they offer a positive and feasible way forward for personalisation that challenges the ambiguities now so often associated with it and restores to it the potential to respond properly to people's unique needs and common rights in the context of a commitment to social justice and social inclusion.

References

Association of Directors of Adult Social Services (2010) *Making resources work in a financial environment*, London: ADASS.

Audit Commission (2010) *Financial management aspects of personal budgets*, London: Audit Commission.

Barclay Committee (1982) *Social workers: their role and tasks (The Barclay Report)*, London: Bedford Square Press.

Batmanghelidjh, C. (2011) 'Big Society can't replace professionals', *London se1*, 8 February. Available at: http://www.london-se1.co.uk/news/view/5091 (accessed 21 November 2011).

Beresford, P. (1982) 'A service for clients', in T. Philpot (ed) *A new direction for social work: the Barclay Report and its implications*, London: Community Care/IPC Business Press, pp 49–62.

Beresford, P. (2007) 'State of independence: analysing individual budgets', *Society Guardian*, 23 May, p 6.

Beresford, P. (2008a) 'Personal budgets must avoid one size fits all, second thoughts', *Society Guardian*, 23 January, p 4.

Beresford, P. (2008b) 'Whose personalisation? Peter Beresford looks at some of the issues raised by the government's rush to social care personalisation', *Soundings, Journal of Politics and Culture*, no 40 (Winter), pp 8–17.

Beresford, P. (2009a) 'Social care, personalisation and service users: addressing the ambiguities', *Research, policy and planning*, vol 27, no 2, pp 73–84.

Beresford, P. (2009b) *Compass think piece 47: whose personalisation?*, London: Compass.

Beresford, P. (2009c) 'Self-directed support: if we are going to do it, let's do it right', Report of a day conference organised by the London Self-Directed Support Forum, London: London Self-Directed Support Forum.

Beresford, P. (2011a) 'Personalisation: no silver bullet', *Disability Now*, May, pp 14–15.

Beresford, P. (2011b) *Transforming social care: sustaining person-centred support, Findings*, York: Joseph Rowntree Foundation.

Beresford, P. and Croft, S. (1984a) *Patch in perspective: decentralising and democratising social services*, London: Battersea Community Action.

Beresford, P. and Croft, S. (1984b) 'Welfare pluralism: the new face of Fabianism', *Critical Social Policy*, no 9 (Spring), pp 19–39.

Beresford, P. and Croft, S. (1986) *Whose welfare: private care or public services?*, Brighton: Lewis Cohen Urban Studies Centre at University of Brighton.

Beresford, P. and Harding, T. (eds) (1993) *A challenge to change: practical experiences of building user led services*, London: National Institute for Social Work.

Beresford, P., Fleming, J., Glynn, M., Bewley, C., Croft, S., Branfield, F. and Postle, K. (2011) *Supporting people: towards a person-centred approach*, Bristol: Policy Press.

Boxall, C., Beresford, P. and Dowson, S. (2009) 'Selling individual budgets, choice and control: local and global influences on UK social care policy for people with learning difficulties', *Policy & Politics,* vol 37, no 4, pp 499–515.

Brindle, D. (2011) 'Are personal budgets for social care living up to their name?', *Society Guardian*, 22 June, p 4.

Carr, S. (2010a) *Personalisation: a rough guide* (revised edn), Adults' Services SCIE Report 20, London: Social Care Institute for Excellence.

Carr, S. (2010b) *Enabling risk, ensuring safety: self-directed support and personal budgets*, Adults' Services SCIE Report 36, London: Social Care Institute for Excellence.

Carr, S. (2011a) 'Personal budgets and international contexts: lessons from home and abroad', *Journal of Care Services Management*, vol 5, no 1, pp 9–22.

Carr, S. (2011b) 'Sarah Carr replies to Glasby et al, "A Beveridge report for the 21st century?"', *Policy & Politics*, vol 39, no 4, pp 618–21.

Cunningham, I. and Nickson, D. (2011) *Personalisation and its implications for work and employment in the voluntary sector*, Voluntary Sector Social Services Workforce Unit Report, Glasgow: Scottish Centre for Employment Research, Strathclyde University.

—

Cutler, T., Waine, B. and Brehony, K. (2007) 'A new epoch of individualisation? Problems with the personalisation of public sector services', *Public Administration*, vol 85, no 3, pp 847–57.

Davey, V., Fernandez, J.-L., Knapp, M., Vick, N., Jolly, D., Swift, P., Tobin, R., Kendall, J., Ferrie, J., Pearson, C., Mercer, G. and Priestley, M. (2007) *Direct payments: a national survey of direct payments policy and practice*, London: Personal Social Services Research Unit, London School of Economics.

Department of Health (2008) *Local authority circular 1: transforming social care*, London: DH.

Duffy, S. (1996) 'Unlocking the imagination'. Available at: http://www.centreforwelfarereform.org/who-we-are/team/simon-duffy.html (accessed 29 August 2013).

Dunning, J. (2011) 'How bureaucracy is derailing personalisation', *Community Care*, 5 August. Available at: http://www.communitycare.co.uk/Articles/05/08/2011/116873/how-bureaucracy-is-derailing-personalisation.htm (accessed 1 July 2012).

Ferguson, I. (2007) 'Increasing user choice or privatizing risk? The antinomies of personalization', *British Journal of Social Work*, vol 37, no 3, pp 387–403.

Finch, J. and Groves, D. (1980) 'Community care and the family: a case for equal opportunities?', *Journal of Social Policy*, vol 9, pp 487–511.

Finch, J. and Groves, D. (eds) (1983) *A labour of love: women, work and caring*, London: Routledge and Kegan Paul.

Fleming, P. and Spicer, A. (2003) 'Working at a cynical distance: implications for subjectivity, power and resistance', *Organization*, vol 10, no 1, pp 157–79.

Flint, J. (2009) 'Subversive subjects and conditional, earned and denied citizenship', in M. Barnes and D. Prior (eds) *Subversive citizens: power, agency and resistance in public services*, Bristol: Policy Press, pp 83–101.

Forder, J., Jones, K., Glendinning, C., Caiels, J., Welch, E., Baxter, K., Davidson, J., Windle, K., Irvine, A., King, D. and Dolan, P. (2012) 'Evaluation of the personal health budget pilot programme', November, PPSRU University of Kent.

Glasgow City Council (2010) 'Self evaluation questionnaire'. Available at: http://www.scottish.parliament.uk/S4_HealthandSportCommittee/General%20Documents/Glasgow_City_Council.pdf (accessed 1 July 2012).

Glasgow City UNISON (2012) 'Report of members meeting', 19 April.

Glasgow Local News (2012) 'Council speaks up on personalisation'. Available at: http://www.localnewsglasgow.co.uk/2012/03/council-speaks-up-on-personalisation/ (accessed 30 April 2012).

Hadley, R. and Hatch, S. (1981) *Social welfare and the failure of the state: centralised social services and participatory alternatives*, London: George Allen and Unwin.

Hadley, R. and McGrath, M. (eds) (1980) *Going local: neighbourhood social services*, NCVO Occasional Paper 1, London: Bedford Square Press.

Hadley, R., Dale, P. and Sills, P. (1984) *Decentralising social services: a model for change*, London: Bedford Square Press.

Harding, T. and Beresford, P. (eds) (1996) *The standards we expect: what service users and carers want from social services workers*, London: National Institute for Social Work.

Hatton, C. and Waters, J. (2013) *Second national personal budget survey (POET), think local act personal*, May, London: In Control Publications.

Hatton, C., Waters, J., Duffy, S., Senker, J., Crosby, N., Poll, C., Tyson, A., O'Brien, J. and Towell, D. (2008) *A report on In Control's second phase: evaluation and learning 2005–2007*, London: In Control.

Henwood, M. and Hudson, B. (2009) *Keeping it personal: supporting people with multiple and complex needs: a report to the Commission for Social Care Inspection*, London: CSCI.

HM Government (2007) *Putting people first: a shared vision and commitment to the transformation of Adult Care Services*, London: HM Government. Available at: http://www.thurrock.gov.uk/socialcare/publications/pdf/dh_people_first.pdf (accessed 30 April 2012).

Ipsos MORI (2011) *Users of social care personal budgets*, London: Ipsos MORI Social Research Institute.

Land, H. and Himmelweit, S. (2010) *Who cares? Who pays: a report on personalisation in social care prepared for UNISON*, London: UNISON.

—

Langan, M. and Lee, P. (eds) (1989) *Radical social work today: social work in the recession*, London: Hutchinsons.

Leadbeater, C. (1988) 'Power to the person', *Marxism Today*, October, pp 14–19.

Leadbeater, C. (1991a) Whose line is it anyway? *Marxism Today*, July, pp 20–4.

Leadbeater, C. (1991b) Manifesto for the public sector *Marxism Today*, May, pp 20–1.

Leadbeater, C. (1997) *The rise of the social entrepreneur*, London: Demos.

Leadbeater, C. (2004) *Personalisation through participation: a new script for public services*, London: Demos.

Leadbeater, C. (2008) 'This time its personal', *Society Guardian*, 16 January, p 6.

Leadbeater, C. and Lownsborough, H. (2005) *Personalisation and participation: the future of social care in Scotland*, London: Demos.

Leadbeater, C., Bartlett, J. and Gallagher, N. (2008) *Making it personal*, London: Demos.

London Self-Directed Support Forum (2013) *Making personalisation work in London*, London: Self-Directed Support Forum.

Morris, J. (2004) 'Independent living and community care: a disempowering framework', *Disability and society*, vol 19, no 5, pp 427–42.

Morris, J. (2005) *Citizenship and disabled people: a scoping paper prepared for the Disability Rights Commission*, London: DRC.

Morris, J. (2011) 'Rethinking disability policy'. Available at: http://www.jrf.org.uk/sites/files/jrf/disability-policy-equality-summary.pdf

NAO (National Audit Office) (2011) *Oversight of user choice and provider competition in care markets*, London: National Audit Office.

Needham, C. (2011a) 'Personalisation: from storyline to practice', *Social Policy & Administration*, vol 45, no 1, pp 54–68.

Needham, C. (2011b) *Personalising public services: understanding the personalisation narrative*, Bristol: Policy Press.

Oliver, M. and Barnes, C. (1998) *Disabled people and social policy: from exclusion to inclusion*, London: Longmans.

OPM (Office for Public Management) (2012) *Longitudinal study of personal budgets for adult social care in Essex, final report*, September, London: Office for Public Management.

Poll, C., Duffy, S., Hatton, S., Sanderson, H. and Routledge, M. (2006) *A report on In Control's first phase 2003–2005*, London: In Control.

Pykett, J. (2009) 'Personalisation and de-schooling: uncommon trajectories in contemporary education policy', *Critical Social Policy*, vol 29, no 3, pp 374–97.

Riddell, S., Pearson, C., Jolly, D., Barnes, C., Priestley, M. and Mercer, G. (2005) 'The development of direct payments in the UK: implications for social justice', *Social Policy & Society*, vol 4, no 1, pp 75–85.

Rose, D., Fleischmann, P., Tonkiss, F., Campbell, P. and Wykes, T. (2002) *User and carer involvement in change management in a mental health context: review of the literature – report to the National Co-ordinating Centre for NHS Service Delivery and Organisation R & D (NCCSDO)*, London: NCCSDO.

Roulstone, A. and Morgan, H. (2009) 'Neo-liberal individualism or self directed support: are we all speaking the same language on modernising adult social care?', *Social Policy and Society*, no 8, pp 333–45.

Rummery, K. (2006) 'Disabled citizens and social exclusion: the role of direct payments', *Policy & Politics*, vol 34, no 4, pp 633–50.

Samuel, M. (2008) 'Social care experiencing "its most important year"', *Community Care*, 31 July, pp 4–5.

Scottish Government (2009) *Changing lives – personalisation: a shared understanding, commissioning for personalisation, & a personalised commissioning approach to support and care services*, Edinburgh: Scottish Government, Service Development Group. Available at: http://www.scotland.gov.uk/Publications/2009/04/07112629/0 (accessed 1 July 2012).

Scottish Parliament (2012) 'Discussion between carers and MSPs'. Available at: http://www.scottish.parliament.uk/S4_HealthandSportCommittee/General%20Documents/Discussion_between_carers_and_MSPs_from_Health_and_Sport_Committee(1).pdf (accessed 1 July 2012).

—

Scourfield, P. (2007) 'Social care and the modern citizen: client, consumer, service user, manager and entrepreneur', *British Journal of Social Work*, vol 37, no 1, pp 107–22.

Self Directed Support Ideas Factory (2009) 'Personalisation and the workforce – the emerging evidence base', Pdf presentation, 17 November.

Series, L. and Clements, L. (2013) 'Putting the cart before the horse: resource allocation systems and community care', *Journal of Social Welfare and Family Law*, vol 35, no 2, pp 207–226.

Skills for Care (2012) *The size and structure of the adult social care sector and workforce in England in 2012*, London: Skills for Care.

Slasberg, C., Beresford, P. and Schofield, P. (2012a) 'Can personal budgets really deliver better outcomes for all at no cost, reviewing the evidence, costs and quality', *Disability & Society*, vol 27, no 7, pp 1029–34.

Slasberg, C., Beresford, P. and Schofield, P. (2012b) 'How self-directed support is failing to deliver personal budgets and personalisation', *Research Policy and Planning,* vol 29, no 3, pp 161–77.

Slasberg, C., Beresford, P. and Schofield, P. (forthcoming [a]) 'How self-directed support is failing to deliver personal budgets and personalisation: an update and refreshed conclusions', *Policy Planning and Research*.

Slasberg, C., Beresford, P. and Schofield, P. (forthcoming [b]) 'The increasing evidence of how self-directed support is failing to deliver personal budgets and personalisation: issues and implications', *Research Policy and Planning*.

Social Value Lab (2012) *Personalisation: readiness and capacity to respond, a survey of providers in Glasgow*, Research Report, May, Glasgow: Social Value Lab.

Stainton, T. and Boyce, S. (2004) '"I have got my life back": users' experience of direct payments', *Disability & Society*, vol 19, no 5, pp 443–54.

Stansfield, J. (2013) 'Are social care personal budgets working?', *The Guardian*. Available at: http://www.guardian.co.uk/society/2013/feb/12/are-social-care-personal-budgets-working (accessed 29 August 2013).

TLAP (Think Local Act Personal) (2011) *Minimum process framework*, October, London: Department of Health.

UNISON Scotland (2011a) 'Social care staff facing pay cuts of up to 23 per cent prepare to strike, says UNISON', 5 September. Available at: http://www.unison-scotland.org.uk/news/2011/septoct/0509.htm (accessed 1 July 2012).

UNISON Scotland (2011b) 'Personalisation in Scotland: the facts'. Available at: http://www.unison-scotland.org.uk/socialwork/Personalisation_01_2012.pdf (accessed 29 August 2013).

UNISON Scotland (2012) 'UNISON submission on the Social Care (Self-directed Support) (Scotland) Bill'. Available at: http://www.scottish.parliament.uk/S4_HealthandSportCommittee/General%20Documents/SDS093_UNISON.pdf (accessed 1 July 2012).

UPIAS (Union of Physically Impaired Against Segregation) (1975) *Fundamental principles of disability*, London: UPIAS/The Disability Alliance.

Waters, J. and Duffy, S. (2007) *Individual budget integration: an exploration of the possible scope of individual budgets, a report for the Department of Health by In Control*, London: In Control.

Whitfield, D. (2012) *In place of austerity: reconstructing the economy, state and public services*, Nottingham: Spokesman.

Williams, D. (2012) 'Copy of David Williams' speech'. Available at: http://www.socialcareideasfactory.com/documents/view.php?documentID=299 (accessed 25 August 2012).